"Eddie Mosley is the real deal! More than bookworm philosopher, Eddie lives and breathes group life. This intensely practical resource will help group leaders and group pastors alike. Eddie shares his heart, his passion, and his experience. You will turn to this book again and again."

—BILL SEARCH, groups pastor, Southeast Christian Church, Louisville, Kentucky

"Through personal learning and real-life experiences, God has blessed Eddie with helpful insights for anyone who desires to connect and equip people for eternal impact. This book is the 'real deal' and a great resource of encouragement to people in the trenches leading group-life communities."

—LAVERNE WEBER, area pastor, Willow Creek Community Church, South Barrington, Illinois

CONNECTING IN COMMUNITIES

UNDERSTANDING THE DYNAMICS OF SMALL GROUPS

EDDIE MOSLEY

NAVPRESS⬤

Discipleship Inside Out™

NAVPRESS
Discipleship Inside Out™

NavPress is the publishing ministry of The Navigators, an international Christian organization and leader in personal spiritual development. NavPress is committed to helping people grow spiritually and enjoy lives of meaning and hope through personal and group resources that are biblically rooted, culturally relevant, and highly practical.

For a free catalog go to www.NavPress.com
or call 1.800.366.7788 in the United States or 1.800.839.4769 in Canada.

© 2011 by Eddie Mosley

ISBN-13: 978-1-61521-685-7

Cover design by Arvid Wallen
Cover photo by Shutterstock/Péter Gudella

While some stories are intentionally vague, all are included with the permission of the persons involved. Any other illustrations are composites of real situations, and any resemblance to people living or dead is coincidental.

Unless otherwise identified, all Scripture quotations in this publication are taken from The Holy Bible, English Standard Version (ESV), copyright © 2001 by Crossway Bibles, a division of Good News Publishers. Used by permission. All rights reserved. Other versions used include: the *Holy Bible, New International Version*® (NIV®), Copyright © 1973, 1978, 1984 by International Bible Society, used by permission of Zondervan, all rights reserved.

Library of Congress Cataloging-in-Publication Data

Mosley, Eddie.
  Connecting in communities : understanding the dynamics of small groups / Eddie Mosley.
      p. cm.
  Includes bibliographical references (p.   ).
  ISBN 978-1-61521-685-7
  1. Small groups--Religious aspects--Christianity. 2. Church group work. I. Title.
  BV652.2.M67 2011
  253'.7--dc22
                                        2010042707
Printed in the United States of America

1 2 3 4 5 6 7 8 / 15 14 13 12 11

To Graham and Gresham,
for vacuuming and cleaning the house for small-group meetings at our place.

To Lisa,
for all the cooking and your steady faith that has calmed me on many occasions.

To Mom and Dad,
for being stable Christ followers all these years and for your many nights of praying for me.

And a special thanks to Mawmaw, Pauline Burba (1935–2009),
who spent her life in community – and showed me what that really means.

CONTENTS

FOREWORD

About every two to three years something new emerges in the world of small groups. I have been observing these innovations and variations for about twenty-five years. Among them are churchwide group strategies, novel approaches to connecting people in life-changing community, innovative DVD curriculum, creative leadership development tools, small-group campaign ideas, and fresh approaches to building groups that are both missional and transformational.

As I read these new ideas and innovations I must say that generally I am thrilled. Having labored in this vineyard many years, it is exciting to see the communal DNA of the church expressed with fresh energy and enthusiasm. Groups, teams, communities, missional hubs, triads, clusters, small groups—whatever the name and however it emerges—new expressions of group life are evidence that Christ is alive and his Spirit is working anew.

But I also have to ask myself some very poignant questions when I look at new models and ideas—the same questions I am asked as I consult with churches and equip leaders around the world. Does this make sense? Does this really work? Will it work in our church? Will my group benefit from this wisdom? Is the author giving me vision hype, describing a reality that is hoped for but does not really exist, except in the author's mind? Or is this the real deal?

The only way to know what's worth your time and attention is to watch the leader and the strategy over time, ask the people who are implementing the strategy, and see the fruit that is borne. Shake the tree. Are any plastic apples falling off? Or is this real fruit? Only then will you see the good, the bad, and the ugly. Sadly, some leaders only offer us hype, endlessly vision-casting a kind of community utopia where everyone is connected, happy, growing, excited, serving, healthy, and transformed. Welcome to "Little Group on the Prairie." Makes for good reading but lousy ministry.

The real world of group life in the local church is vastly different. And that is where Eddie Mosley and his team have been slugging it out, building groups and sharing what they have learned. After all, Eddie is a learner, like every good leader worth his or her salt. He is not so proud that he cannot glean from and integrate the expertise and wisdom of others; and he is not so naive as to uncritically consume every new model that bursts onto the scene, swallowing it hook, line, and sinker, foolishly implementing it without vigorous critique.

As you will see from the pages that follow, Eddie is an experienced convener. He brings together people, ideas, strategies, and experiences from a range of group models and churches, adapts them, adds his own, and then shares what has worked. He does not claim to have discovered something new when it is not, and he speaks simply and directly, graciously offering his church experience as a kind of a petri-dish experiment we can observe and analyze.

I hope this book inspires lots of other "Eddies" out there — innovative yet humble leaders, who strive and sweat, listen and learn, labor and love each day to build authentic, redemptive communal life in and through the local church. I hope you dissect the material, challenge the assumptions, test the ideas, and pester Eddie with endless e-mails and calls. *(Sorry, Eddie, but when you decide to share your opinions and decisions in writing, it comes with the territory! You'll love it.)*

What you have before you are the collective insights and experiences of a leader-learner who has been navigating the process of building group life in the local church for many years. I trust you steward this resource well. Ask other team members to read it, then get together and talk it through over a long lunch. Let it stimulate your thinking, refine your present strategy, and open your minds to some fresh ideas. You'll be a better leader for it.

BILL DONAHUE

best-selling author of *Leading Life-Changing Small Groups*, speaker and group life consultant at www.drbilldonahue.com

AUTHOR'S NOTE

My view of small groups has been developing for many more years than I realized. I have always thought they were a lot like family. You know — the drama, the kids, the EGR (extra-grace-required person), and the parent who leads the way.

I am an only child, so there were never more than ten people at our Christmas family dinner, and we opened our gifts one person at a time. Yes, we even saved the bows and some of the paper. At our Thanksgiving dinner there might be four or five people total. We could all eat at one table and have one conversation going; it was a very calm event.

But when I got married I was thrust into a large family. My first Christmas with my in-laws included six siblings and their spouses, twenty-six grandchildren, plus cousins that I did not even know. All the grandchildren opened their gifts all at the same time, and paper and bows were thrown everywhere.

My first Thanksgiving dinner at my in-laws was another life-changing experience, with approximately fifty people attending. It wasn't even on Thanksgiving Day, because in order to have most of the family in attendance we had to pick a neutral date and time. I sat next to someone I had never met, while family members ate in several different rooms. Conversations and people would drift from room to room as we discussed life, health, babies and loss of babies, marriage and divorce, finances and farming. Kids of all ages ran in and out of the house laughing, playing, crying, and wanting more "mashed taties." The conversation, care, and growth never stopped, nor were they interrupted by the kids.

Small groups are a lot like Thanksgiving at Mamaw's house. You never know who is going to be there, what subjects may come up, or what life issues may be revealed—but you do know you can share, speak your mind, be loved and cared for, and be invited back.

While the stories, principles, and practices shared in this book are from real-life experiences of small groups based out of a local church, this view has helped me with the bigger picture of life in God's world. Ministry is not always clean, pretty, or fun, but you can keep the perspective and objectives clear. And by this clarity and focus on the goal, lives will be transformed and communities impacted.

THE JOURNEY OF A SMALL-GROUP LEADER AND PASTOR

What in the world is God doing? If you have journeyed as a Christ follower for any length of time, you have probably pondered this question. As I look back over my many years as a Christian—from a country boy on the farm to a staff member at a megachurch in suburban America—I think about all the times I've asked this question. This is the reason Jeremiah 29:11 has been a guiding scripture for my life: "You have no clue what God has planned next for you, but know that it is good" (my paraphrase). Despite my ignorance as to God's next step for my life, I have had the privilege and honor to serve him in churches of various size in the southeast United States and have seen him develop a plan and a people-oriented small-group ministry that is seeing lives transformed and communities impacted.

In a small group, people study the Bible together and discuss the issues and challenges of life. They pray, care for one another, and are missed if they don't show up. Friendships form. Small groups transform a large church into a small, intimate congregation. Small groups are organic in nature. That means they operate more as a family, with issues, time constraints, and changes constantly occurring in the lives of their members. Small groups are not a program, scheduled tightly around an academic setting or curriculum; instead, they are more a process of experiencing life together over time, in many settings, in all situations. I believe small group is the best place for sustained life change to occur.

Small groups have a powerful impact on lives and communities. Yet they are not a simple process to design or implement in every church. Through the seven chapters of this book you will see how basic principles, lived out through a focused strategy, including intentional sharing of the stories, have impacted people and communities.

For the last several years I have served on staff at LifePoint Church in Smyrna, Tennessee. Although this church is one hundred years old, the name was changed in 2009 to represent our culture and the worldwide impact to which God was leading us. LifePoint's GroupLife Ministry is less than eight years in the making, but God has used this ministry to transform many lives, families, and our community.

The stories and practices in *Connecting in Communities* have been lived out in the local church for many years. And I was blessed to have some great small-group leaders walk before me in the LifePoint GroupLife Ministry. They led with a strong passion for having a plan, objectives, and true transparent community. They determined the objectives used at LifePoint—Discipleship, Community, and Service—that we have spent the last few years communicating, and this is the vision others can rally around.

WITH OR OF SMALL GROUPS

LifePoint has evolved from a church with some study groups following the Purpose Driven movement in 2003 to a church of small groups. LifePoint Church has developed six core values and five expectations that keep the congregation focused on what God has instructed LifePoint to accomplish. The culture of LifePoint has developed into one that allows us to continue this strong focus on connecting people and experiencing life change. Following the churchwide example of clear expectations and core values, leadership of the small-groups division worked early on to establish three objectives for small groups that keep us focused. The stories you are about to read are results of people living out LifePoint's combination of objectives, expectations, and core values. These are stories of real people connected through small-group life, which is impacting them, their families, their communities, and, ultimately, the world.

My life is now driven by the chance to see this impact take place in small groups, communities, and individual lives. It's my mission—my joy. The search for vision and purpose is not always clean and easy, but when you catch the vision God has for your life you don't need Red Bull or Vault. Your heart beats faster, your blood pressure rises, and your eyes open wider with excitement. The adrenaline gets pumping and you are ready to take on the world.

This vision wakes me up in the middle of the night; the energy jumps into my bones and causes me to learn, read, watch, coach, study, talk, and share. Seeing lives transformed with a hope and a future—nothing does this like relationships. And nothing builds this level of relationship like a small group. It takes a leader to passionately pursue discipleship, community, and service with four or five other couples. These people are in your life, your neighborhood, your small group, your family. They are you! They are leaders and learners. This vision can become a reality in your ministry!

THE JOURNEY BEGINS

The message of *Connecting in Communities* is from my life in ministry, my family, and my life experiences. This message is designed to help you from the perspective of what I have experienced as a small-group pastor, specifically in the small-group ministry of LifePoint church. We have borrowed, adapted, or implemented processes and practices from various churches and published materials. You'll discover how we put all this together to make our small-group ministry become a vital part of our lives as Christ followers.

Intended for pastors, church leadership, and small-group ministers or point persons, *Connecting in Communities* is a practical, hands-on guide to take you from "just talking about it" to actually implementing a small-group ministry. Small-group leaders will benefit from the useful how-to nature of *Connecting in Communities*; it's filled with anecdotes, tips, and small-group wisdom. It will guide you through the journey of life-change stories that result from a focus on true community through small groups. There are basic principles and processes of small-group ministry that have proven to make a difference in lives and communities. The stories will help you understand and know that the ministry of your dreams, the relationships you hope to establish, and the impact that you desire in your community *are possible*. You will learn how to implement these experiences in your own community as God leads you. *Connecting in Communities* is a journey through ministry, community, church, and small groups. Let God show you his plan for your ministry as you learn what has made the difference in others.

SMALL GROUPS IMPACT COMMUNITIES

There are places in the world where Christians tend to live in the same neighborhood, close to each other, perhaps because they are in the minority and living in community is more comfortable or safer. But that's not the case in twenty-first-century America. No matter how involved in church activities you might be, whether you're employed in a staff position or volunteer your leadership skills, at the end of the day you go home to a subdivision or neighborhood in which you might be the only Christ follower for blocks. It is here that your ministry or small group could make the largest impact. The following story is the result of living out the dynamics of small groups.

THE ACCIDENT

It may have happened to you many times. Someone in the community has a car wreck, and you get the call. Most of the time you rush to the hospital to meet with the family and pray with them.

On this busy Tuesday afternoon, something felt different when an e-mail came from my neighborhood's homeowners association (HOA) informing me that a neighbor had been in a serious car accident; he was not injured but in trouble. It was odd for the HOA to contact me about a personal matter with a homeowner. However, I immediately replied, "What should we do?" The answer came back, "The HOA cannot get involved in this type of issue, but we knew you would want to know and possibly minister to the family." I contemplated the issue for the rest of the afternoon because I did not know this neighbor. He lived in a different section of our subdivision and only came by our house when he was riding his four-wheeler.

On the way home that evening I drove by his house and prayed for an opening to talk with him and his family. At supper I told my family about our neighbor and his accident. As was often the case, one of our teenage son's friends had dropped by and joined us at the table. As I continued the story, he piped in and said he knew the man; in fact, he had been four-wheeling with him just hours before the accident. I told him I would love to meet with this man and his family if possible.

Wednesday morning came and when I walked into our office area I was met by one of our assistants. She told me she was a friend of a woman whose husband was in jail from a car accident and that they lived in my subdivision. She searched the church database and discovered the family had visited our church once. That was all I needed to get in the door. I asked her to go with our campus pastor and me to see the family. She asked if we should call first. My immediate response was no, because I did not want the wife to be able to tell us not to come visit.

We loaded up and drove to their home. The wife would not answer the door. Our assistant called her to let her know who was at the door, and only after determining it was not the media, she let us in. The conversation started out light; I told her where I lived and why we were there—as neighbors, as ministers, as friends. It wasn't long before we discovered her daughter had actually been to my house playing with other kids from the neighborhood. For the next hour we compassionately listened as this woman disclosed what had happened and her concern about the future: Her husband had been involved in an injury accident and arrested for allegedly speeding and DUI. They were very worried as they waited on the recovery of the people who had also been in the other car. We prayed with her and offered our help in any way.

My son's friend came by on Friday night and told me the man had gotten out of jail and he wanted to meet with me sometime but would call first. I waited, wondering if I should just drop by his house, but something told me to wait. Two weeks went by before he contacted me. On Sunday I was introduced to him at church, and we set a time for me to come to his house. On Tuesday I went to his house. We talked, and I silently prayed to be clear on where to guide the conversation. He gave his life to Christ right there in his living room. The next hour was full of conversation about discipleship, helping him understand the Bible, church, next steps, and how to talk with his wife about his decision. He did not have a Bible, only the little one his five-year-old daughter had received from vacation Bible school. He knew "it had red letters in it," and he had heard at church last week that "those are the words Jesus used." He was quite embarrassed because he had waited until he was forty-one and something tragic had to happen for him to let God into his life. You could feel the relief in the room, and we both were emotional over what had just happened.

I knew my next step was to discuss water baptism and getting him connected with others at the church—and at LifePoint, that would be via small groups. I listened for my opportunity to introduce both of these. As the discussion continued he mentioned one of my best friends, a fellow baseball coach and small-group leader, Charlie. I knew then that the next step had been clearly planned by the Holy Spirit, and connecting him to a small group would be no problem. He said he would visit Charlie's small group next week. Two weeks later I had the honor and privilege of baptizing him, with his family and many of our neighbors present in the service.

Why would the HOA contact a neighbor when a resident had had a wreck and was in jail? We have spent the last four years encouraging small groups to be involved in their neighborhoods or subdivisions by hosting parties (Easter egg hunts, breakfasts with Santa, food drives, bonfires, firework shows, and so forth) to reestablish neighborhood. Through four years of investing in our subdivision, several people have discovered that I "work at the church." The HOA leaders said it was only natural to contact me when they found out about this situation.

WHAT ABOUT YOUR IMPACT?

Does your church have that kind of influence in the community? Are you aligned so that you can minister to people far from God just because you are active in your community? Are your small-group objectives clear to your group leaders so that they understand their role as a representative of Christ and the church to their community? How can you develop a system in which it is natural to meet the needs in your church and community? How do you go from a church with a successful Sunday school program that reaches those who choose to come to God to a growing small-group ministry that impacts people in your community, your subdivision, your schools, and your city? It is a journey that I can describe best in my own story.

LIFE CHANGE FOR THIS MINISTER

I remember the day it started. The day my life changed from a minister focused on managing a program that enlarged and strengthened the church and helped people know the Bible to a lifestyle that connects people, helps them experience life change, and changes eternity for those around me. I was moving from Tennessee to Kentucky for a new ministry position that allowed me to work from home and network with churches across the state.

As my family and I awaited the completion of our house, a friend gave me a book about community and church — *The Connecting Church* by Randy Frazee.[1] I finished reading it a couple of weeks before we moved in, which allowed time to design the final plans on our house. *The Connecting Church* is about doing things in your life to increase the opportunities to connect with your neighbors. For example, using ideas from the book, we decided not to build a six-foot privacy fence around the backyard; instead, we installed a forty-two-inch picket fence so we could easily have conversations over it with our neighbors. We decided not to buy a treadmill, but to get a puppy and walk the neighborhood. We also stayed home more and invited neighbors over for cookouts and parties.

Prior to this move, my family and I had lived in the same house for almost eight years but did not know our neighbors and had not experienced closeness in a neighborhood before. I was busy at the church, being a father and a husband, and really just wanted to sit in my comfy chair when I got home at night. Besides, most nights I was in a committee meeting at church.

As a new lifestyle began to happen around our new home and neighbors, the idea of small groups kept coming up in conversations and in my new church and new job. I met and became friends with Travis, in whom God was working as well. He and his family had recently joined the same church as my family had, and we began to "do life" together. As we looked around the church, we noticed a lot of young couples for which there was no Bible study class, so we thought about starting one. But we wanted to create something different; we wanted this to be more than a class, more than just a study of the Bible. It would be a group of friends, close friends, who could be transparent with each other and do life together, something that was regular but not programmed. We dreamed of having friends who truly loved and cared for each other—no matter how tough life was or how far we fell from grace, or how goofy we might act. We discovered that there *are* people just like us, hoping, dreaming, searching for the same kind of friends, the same kind of relationships.

Travis and I decided to start a class targeting this age group. The first week he and I rolled into the room and sat for an hour. Just us, just watching people walk by and look in the door. The second week our wives joined us, and, thus, we experienced every class leader's dream—we doubled our group in one week. The third week, his wife was sick so we settled for a class of three, 75 percent of our highest attendance. That Monday our pastor called and offered twenty-two tickets to the skybox of a local minor-league baseball team. With the help of many people at church, we began to invite couples we had met to the game that Saturday night.

It was a big success—ten couples, free food, and baseball from the skybox. During the game I asked each couple if they knew the charge for the ticket. Each quickly responded, "Travis said it was free." I then corrected them, saying, "You have to come to class tomorrow morning!" Everyone laughed. We spent the rest of the game sharing ideas, dreams, stories, and building the relationships.

On Sunday, we had fourteen people in attendance. We were so excited. Although we did not have a goal, objectives, or even plans for the next three weeks, we had *people*—new friends to share the study and application of the Bible. From then on we referred to this experience as Skybox Evangelism.

Over the next three years we developed into a small group—from couples at our church and neighborhoods. We lived out much more than Bible study. We did life together through the week, served and built community with each other. We never dropped below fourteen in our group. Our network grew and the group experienced life together as we served each other, united to help the community. We laughed, cried, suffered, and celebrated together all of life's ups and downs. We realized we had stumbled onto something none of us had ever had—a community of people, connected and experiencing life change in Christ. Then we realized we had to share it.

A lot has changed in my life and the lives of those around me. Those three years of practicing community led to eight families who became friends and helpful neighbors; three fathers were baptized; one boy accepted Christ; a marriage on the rocks became a solid marriage; and God added to his church. I had no idea the eternal impact one person could have just by being involved in his neighborhood. Now I'm a small-group evangelist, and my mission comes straight from Scripture.

This concept of small groups impacting community is found in Acts 2:42-47:

> And they devoted themselves to the apostles' teaching and the fellowship, to the breaking of bread and the prayers. And awe came upon every soul, and many wonders and signs were being done through the apostles. And all who believed were together and had all things in common. And they were selling their possessions and belongings and distributing the proceeds to all, as any had need. And day by day, attending the temple together and breaking bread in their homes, they received their food with glad and generous hearts, praising God and having favor with all the people. And the Lord added to their number day by day those who were being saved.

These verses motivate me to try to multiply this experience over and over in my life, my community, and my church. And as God developed this passion, this mission, this life in my heart, he was also preparing a position in a church for me. In May 2005 I rejoined the talented team of ministers at LifePoint Church. And over the last few years I have enjoyed watching the development and growth of our small-group ministry and its impact in our community.

SMALL-GROUP LEADER

Living out this vision as a church minister was a little different. My family and I joined a small group for a few months when we came back to LifePoint. Then I stepped out and started a new small group with a group of new people. As a small-group leader, I was passionate about seeing people come to Christ and grow in their relationship with him.

My family and I were part of our second small group

when I realized there were other LifePoint attendees who lived in my subdivision. We talked together about hosting a neighborhood fireworks show, since each of us knew of neighbors who'd spent a lot of money on fireworks the previous Fourth of July but seemed to shoot them almost as a competition. We contacted these neighbors and asked if they would be willing to combine their fireworks for a massive subdivision show. They all agreed and on the fourth we threw a big cookout party with a bonfire and fireworks. Before the fireworks started, people were introducing themselves and telling where they lived. As I made my way through the large crowd, I listened for any sign of or lack of spiritual conversation or words.

A few of the neighbors knew I was on staff at LifePoint; they made a point of introducing me to other families who had revealed that they attended LifePoint. I met twelve families that night who seemed open to the idea of attending a cookout at my house in a couple of weeks. I told them that the cookout was to discuss maybe having a Bible study at my house. Eight of those families showed up for the cookout, and seven of them committed to attending a six-week discussion/study on parenting. I found it very interesting that only four of these families actually attend a church. So there we were starting a neighborhood small group—and half the group was unchurched.

We were a group for a little over six months. At some point we discussed other subdivision residents we had befriended over the last few months. Wondering if they would be interested in being in a small group, one of the couples in our group hosted an open house and each of us invited more neighbors. Within a few months we had two small groups meeting in our subdivision.

THE CHURCH'S ROLE

As executive director of GroupLife, the small-group ministry at LifePoint, I also have the opportunity and responsibility to enlist small-group leaders, design an organization that grows more leaders, develop these leaders, and multiply the ministry. To learn and understand how to help others experience what I was experiencing in my neighborhood small group, I began to network with other small-group pastors across the country. I contacted the three biggest churches I knew to see if anyone might have time to mentor or coach me. Willow Creek (in the Chicago area) was very open to my learning from them by attending their small-groups conference. Randy Frazee was gracious enough to tell me about his neighborhood ministry through Willow Creek. While there I also met LaVerne Weber, who was guiding the neighborhood ministers under Randy's leadership. LaVerne told me about the impact neighborhood ministry was having and encouraged me to continue on the journey of establishing neighborhood ministry.

I also traveled to North Point (Atlanta area) to review their GroupLink assimilation process led by Bill Willits. GroupLink is a concept first discussed by Andy Stanley and Bill Willits in their book *Creating Community* and used with much success at North Point Church in Alpharetta, Georgia.[2] Bill took the time to explain every aspect of GroupLink to me. It is a method to connect church visitors and members to a small group if they are not currently participating in one. This concept has also been adapted by LifePoint Church for the same purpose.

Then I was off to Saddleback Church in Orange County, California, where Steve Gladen is small-groups pastor. Steve helped me understand the purposes of small groups, as well as leadership development. I could see that each of these people was being used of God in developing neighborhood, assimilation, and small-group ministry. They were also quick to help a young minister who was trying to learn.

Each of their ministries had similarities, and I worked with our team for several months to adapt their successes into a plan we could use at LifePoint. We also continued to learn from other churches and leaders. Rick Rusaw was one of the first speakers at our annual small-group leaders banquet. He was asked to speak after a friend gave me his book *The Externally Focused Church*. The theme of Rick's book is: "If your church vanished, would your community notice, weep? Would anyone notice? Would anyone care?"[3] A personalization from the theme of the book kept running through my mind: "If our church vanished, would Smyrna notice?" I believed if we took the gospel to the neighborhoods via small groups, the answer would be yes. I also felt that I had to apply Rick's theme to my life and home: "If I moved, would anyone on my street even notice?" Rusaw inspired many at the banquet that night to make a difference not only in their groups and communities but also to challenge the church to take the lead.

To get started, we purchased Microsoft MapPoint to map our entire congregation and see where God was at work. At that time, LifePoint was probably no different from your church. Most of the members lived in close proximity to the church, roughly a three-mile radius. In that radius were several subdivisions, but no representation of ministry other than church members who lived there. There was no type of ongoing focus to make a difference on any particular street. We identified the location of the small groups that were already meeting. Next, we mapped members and attendees close to the location of these small groups. We encouraged the small-group leaders to contact nearby LifePoint members or attendees and invite them to a cookout or dessert party. The party was to see if they wanted to participate in a Bible study in that neighborhood and/or help throw quarterly block parties for all the neighbors. And now we have an answer to the question Rick Rusaw posed: We can confidently say, for several of our neighborhoods, if our church vanished from the community, people would definitely notice.

ADOPT A SCHOOL

Another way our small groups are impacting the community is by adopting their local public school. Small-group leaders are taking the initiative to contact the closest school to discover needs. One of the most unique stories that developed from this strategy was actually initiated by an eighth grade class. We now call it the Pig Letter Story.

It all started when I received a couple of letters from students at a local middle school. Their teacher had asked them to write a persuasive business letter that would generate donations to buy a pig for people in Africa via the Heifer Project. The charity was chosen because of its unblemished reputation. The Heifer Project is a nonprofit charitable organization based in Little Rock, Arkansas, dedicated to relieving global hunger and poverty. It provides gifts of livestock and plants, as well as education in sustainable agriculture, to financially disadvantaged families around the world.[4]

It was a joy to receive the two letters. Then another coworker came to my office with two more letters from different students; then someone else came in with five more letters from other students; then another staff member came in with four more letters. In the end we had thirteen letters from this mini-school of eighth graders, asking us to donate large or small amounts to help them raise $120 to purchase a pig for a family in Africa.

LifePoint is known as a mission-minded, sending church. Each year we send many mission teams across America and around the world to share Christ and help with health and educational needs. Africa is one of the countries we send teams to several times each year. So the letters had a bigger emotional impact than the students realized. A few staff members got together and discussed how to help the students in a larger way than just sending a few dollars.

We decided to share the Pig Story with all of the small groups at LifePoint. This was an opportunity to support the students, to partner with a teacher and a school, and to make a lifelong impression on each life as to the power of influence.

The church's evangelism strategy is modeled after Andy Stanley's "Invest to Invite," in which you build relationships with people who are far from God. Once invested in that relationship, you watch for the opportunity to use your influence for Christ as well as share your story. The persuasive letters we received reminded us of the power of influence. So we jumped on the idea to spread this opportunity.

Over the next two weeks there was a unique excitement around the LifePoint offices and small groups about how much money we had raised for the Pig Letter. Our hallways were a little more alive and filled with laughter as someone would yell out, "Another Pig Letter!"

Small groups collected over $800 for the pig. I had the honor of delivering the check to the school; the teacher asked me to speak to each of the classes in the mini-school. I asked why so many students had sent the letter to LifePoint (thinking the teacher had suggested it or perhaps one of the students started it as a joke). But a couple of the students spoke up and said, "We know your church is about helping people." This was a humbling moment. When I said, "Thank you for letting us be a part of your project," the teacher and students thanked me for LifePoint Church and the impact we are making on the students and around the world.

Since the experience of the Pig Letter, small groups are now taking the initiative to contact their local schools and build a relationship with counselors, principals, and teachers to partner in making their communities better and closer in relationship. Each small group is expected to have an ongoing service project. Many of them are choosing the school that their own members' children attend. And thus community impact happens.

EXAMPLES OF COMMUNITY

One of the examples of community we use at LifePoint to help people catch the vision is a clip from the movie *Christmas with the Kranks*. In this film, Vic Frohmeyer, a somewhat nosy neighbor, comes to the rescue of the Kranks when he discovers their daughter is returning home for Christmas. The Kranks (empty nesters now) have decided to skip Christmas and take a cruise instead; they've even declined to decorate their house and yard, and their neighbors aren't pleased about it. On several occasions Vic and other concerned neighbors confront Mr. or Mrs. Krank on the issue, but the Kranks are determined to skip Christmas. But when they learn that their daughter is coming home for their annual neighborhood Christmas party, panic ensues. Neighbors are none too excited to help the Kranks, but Vic steps in with a dramatic speech given from the back bumper of an ambulance: "All right, people, listen up, gather round. We're about to have a party here at the Kranks', a Christmas homecoming for Blair. Drop what you're doing and pitch in. Nora, do you have a turkey? Anybody got a turkey?" A lady from the crowd responds, "I have two." "Beautiful, get 'em," Vic replies. A frustrated man in the crowd yells back, "Hold on, why should we do this for him?" and others in the crowd chime in, "Yeah, he's a jerk!" Vic brings the crowd to silence as he casts the vision for the event. "Regardless of how you feel about Luther, I know a lot of you have mixed feelings about him now. But we're a community and the people in a community stick together." As the crowd disbands to prepare the party, Luther's wife turns to the crowd and says, "Thank you."[5]

Not only is this the neighborhood we are seeing develop among some small groups, it is also an example of the community we all want to experience. Who wouldn't want neighbors to rally around when he is down? Who wouldn't want someone to step up and say, "We will help"?

SHARING THE STORIES

We were able to get more people to join in the vision of small group and neighborhood by sharing stories. We took every opportunity we could to tell anyone who would listen what was taking place in a few of our small groups. Neighborhood stories made it into our local paper and we would post these on our wall, in our blogs, and link to them in e-mails.

The excitement began to grow through the staff, members, and attendees of LifePoint Church.

Neighborhood ministry and small groups started gaining a following at LifePoint as the stories were shared in the halls, in meetings, and in baptism videos. I enumerated stories every week in staff meeting of things we were doing and the lives that were being affected by this focus on neighborhood. After twelve months of hearing story after story, our executive pastor Kyle Goen spoke up and disclosed that he'd drawn a map of his street. On it he'd marked every house and who lived there; to his surprise, he was only able to put names with three of the twelve homes on his street. He then declared he was going to plant a garden in the side yard so he could be out more and speak to his neighbors as they went by. And he did. As the garden grew over the next few months, he delivered vegetables to the neighbors he did not know. It wasn't an easy decision to start to establish neighborhood relationships, but he stayed the course and in one summer had conversations with most of the families on his street.

In the story of the rich young man told in Matthew 19:16-19, Jesus was asked, "Teacher, what good deed must I do to have eternal life?" And Jesus said, "Keep the commandments. . . . Love your neighbor as yourself" (paraphrased). This verse serves as a daily reminder of the impact we are to have on our street and through our church. Ministry is not just about numbers or a process; it is so much more. As a small-group leader or small-group point person, you have a great opportunity to influence your community. Begin today to notice the people around you. Be sensitive to the conversations and opportunities God is giving you. Watch for opportunities to tell the story of life change; stories are all around us, happening every day in the good times, in tragedies, and on your street. You will be surprised when people begin to listen and even celebrate with you.

STORIES: IN THE TRAGEDIES

I was working on e-mail about 5:30 one Tuesday morning when someone knocked on our front door. Coffee in hand, I answered and found one of my neighbors. She had tragic news about a young boy, the son of her close friend, who had been killed the night before in a car accident. I was in shock, yet immediately thought about the neighborhood the family lived in and the many small groups from LifePoint Church that are housed in that same neighborhood.

As she left my house, I thought about the best plan for mobilizing the ministry that would need to take place for this family. Around 8:30 I called the small-group coordinator for that area. He had not heard about the accident yet but said he would make some calls. In a few minutes he called back and said that everything was under way; the family was being cared for by two small groups in the neighborhood. I felt relieved that our system of networks and neighborhoods had worked.

What I did not realize at first was that those small groups had gone to work about 8:00, at least thirty minutes before the official call came from my office. Wow—how did that happen? This is how: The neighborhood small groups are so close that when one neighbor heard the terrible news, she called the small-group leaders (not the pastor, not the GroupLife pastor, not the coordinator—but her *neighbors*). By the time I had done what I thought was getting the ball rolling, they had already been in the home and prepared food for the family.

STORIES: WHERE YOU LIVE

"Where you live," said LaVerne Weber in a forum I attended at Willow Creek, "is as important as how you serve, what you give, and attendance you count." When I heard it, I began to think about what this really meant to my life, my ministry, and my family. It was not long before I began to understand that you may have bought a house because you liked it and it was a good deal, but it was no accident—that good deal was one God put together for a reason.

Starbucks has a career-opportunity card that reads, "Create Community. Make a difference in someone's day." Flip it over and you'll see, "When you work at Starbucks, you can make a difference in someone's day by creating an environment where neighbors and friends can get together and reconnect while enjoying a great coffee experience."[6] Coffee, which is their business, is almost the last word in the message. Starbucks points its employees to a different focus: making a *difference*, not a cup of coffee.

Where you live is no accident. Individualism and isolation are things of the past for those of us practicing ministry in our neighborhoods. Where you live is a place that God has placed you—to be the presence of Jesus. You can walk the streets with excitement. You can wave to neighbors as they drive by your house. You can partner with other neighbors to plan neighborhood parties and events. Where you live is not just where you sleep and eat; your house isn't just a structure you work long hours to pay for. Your home is a place of *peace*, a place of *encouragement*, a place of *smiles* and *friendliness* for all neighbors, a place someone can come and *sit a while* and *share* and *receive* the unconditional love of Christ through your family. Your house is a place for stories to be heard, discussed, and written. Go home today and begin to write a story of God's impact on your street. Find neighbors who are open to learn about God and proclaim his love to others.

These stories are the result of practicing the dynamics explained in this book. The result of people connecting in communities can have impact far beyond the local church. *Connecting in Communities* can impact your neighborhood as you live out the dynamics explained herein. The following chapters will show how your church, your ministry, and your small group can impact your community, step by step. This is how a small-group ministry begins.

A Block Party

We had a chili cook-off at the [neighborhood] common area. We just put a flyer on everyone's door asking them to call if they planned on competing in the chili cook-off on Saturday night. There were fifteen pots of chili, some hot, some sweet, and one designed by four teenagers labeled VERY HOT! We had judges and awarded prizes, and even rented an inflatable for the kids. People stayed later than we thought and had to walk home in the dark — but they had fun. We are now planning a Thanksgiving re-gift event to help the local shelters.

— Benjamin B.

FIVE PRACTICAL STEPS FOR . . .

Small-Group Point Person:

1. Map your membership.
2. Host a neighborhood party with others from your church and/or start a neighborhood small group.
3. Identify current classes or groups who might adopt a school for a semester.
4. Read Rick Rusaw's book *The Externally Focused Church* and Randy Frazee's book *The Connecting Church*.
5. Listen for stories you can tell about, along with your own story. Share them *often*.

Small-Group Leader:

1. Map your neighborhood by drawing the streets and houses. Now draw a route you can use on a daily after-dinner walk or to walk your dog.
2. Host a neighborhood block party as a group.
3. Discuss adopting a local school with your group. Identify the

point person from your group to contact the school concerning needs your group might meet.

4. Read Rick Rusaw's book *The Externally Focused Church* and discuss it as a small group.

5. Pass on stories about your group's service or neighborhood impact to other small-group leaders.

WHAT DO I DO FIRST?

Small groups should not be defined by size, when they meet, what they produce, or what they study; instead, they should be defined by the objectives of what they aim to accomplish. For example, you've just read about small groups making a difference in their own neighborhoods. But the level of small-group ministry discussed in the previous chapter is not easy to attain. It takes a focused objective.

The buzzword *small group* is sweeping the nation and now you or your pastor wants to jump on board. You attend the latest conference and cannot wait to implement all the new ideas you hear. But before jumping in with both feet, there are questions you should ask about the objectives. If you have had small groups in your church for several years, the questions posed in this chapter will remind you why you started small groups and may serve to remind you of the foundational principles for which you started them. If you are considering starting small groups in your church, these questions will help you design a firm foundation for small groups.

One church's story may help you see the questions and steps for developing this culture of small-group ministry. After hearing about the wave of small groups springing up in churches across the nation, the minister of education and his staff began to ask questions about starting small groups at their church. The staff had several conversations, and then the minister of education called me. I knew this man; we had met several years earlier through a Southern Baptist Convention network. We discussed all the benefits and struggles of adding small groups to a church that has had success with Sunday school. He asked all the usual questions about counting attendance, curriculum control, child care, and connection and support to the local church. Since small groups would not meet on-campus, these were issues that concerned him greatly. We talked for about forty-five minutes with the conversation getting heated at some points due to these major concerns. At the end of the phone call I was not sure if he would ever call again.

About a month later he called back and said his staff would love to sit and talk about church culture and small groups; they wanted to discuss the limitations they were experiencing at their church. He asked me to come to their staff retreat to discuss the culture at LifePoint and how small groups were helping not only in the numerical growth but also in the discipleship of many adults. They were interested in the possibility of enlarging the number of adults in Bible study without having to build more buildings.

After that spring retreat, the staff was excited to give small groups a try. We mapped out a calendar for the next three months, and they began by piloting six small groups, each led by a staff person.

Eleven months after our initial phone conversation, I received an e-mail update. "Let me update and clarify our group activity to date. We call our small groups Community Groups. We have followed Eddie's suggested timeline [see the appendix]. During the summer we started our pilots and had six groups. In the fall we grew to ten. In planning for our spring campaign, we had over forty groups committed in the study. We had thirteen groups participating in GroupLink. The other twenty-seven groups either had their groups filled or are pursuing other participants without the aid of GroupLink. This was exciting and the enemy threw in some warfare. Our goal was to keep these groups going after the campaign ends. Our goal was 80 percent retention. We also asked each group to have a service day. We asked all small groups involved in the study to do a one and a half-hour service activity in their community."[1]

That's quite an accomplishment. By the time the churchwide campaign started, this church had more than fifty groups participating. In one year, this church went from learning about small groups to having more than four dozen of them; on average, that is five hundred adults in Bible study. Many of them had not previously been connected to a Bible study group; in fact, some of them were not even connected to the church.

This story is the result of many conversations and a master plan, which was patient and well thought out. The church leadership had to be informed and voice support for this pilot project season before the dream of success could be realized. The pastor had to be on board, or at least open to the idea of small groups. The staff had to be united on the pilot project and not see it as competition to their individual ministries. Out of the pilot groups there were stories to share. Much prayer went into discovering who to invite to the pilot groups. The intentional apprenticing process had to be made clear up front. Everyone from the pilot groups would either lead a group or assist leading a group in the fall. Then, as the momentum grew through sharing stories from group life, the staff and church were ready for a churchwide spring campaign inviting everyone to participate.

How can your church experience such a mass movement into small groups? How can you increase your success in starting small groups so that more people are discipled?

The journey of starting groups in your church is not a quick fix. A healthy church and staff team is, obviously, beneficial to any new opportunity's success. But the success is based on more than a healthy staff. It requires prayer, planning, relationships, and a culture that is open to trying something new.

For many years you and I have heard stories of a minister who travels to a conference, hears some great stories and ministry ideas, and then returns home to implement all these new grand ideas. What he or she failed to hear (or weren't told) is the story of the years of work, sleepless nights, days in prayer, months (maybe years) of transitioning the culture that the example church had been going through. Sure, it was all running smoothly at the time of the conference. What the attendee may have also missed is that God had that plan for the first church, but he had an adaption of the plan in mind for the second church. Many ministers have been called into some difficult conversations because they've tried to implement all the programs and processes they heard at a conference.

I receive a phone call a couple times a month from a minister of education or small-groups pastor who is considering starting small groups or changing how they do small groups. I discuss with him how I started in small-group ministry, the mistakes I made (forcing the program of small groups, not piloting, pushing people to join rather than establishing relationships), the decisions that were obviously of God, and the people who have grown and changed to be more like Christ because of small groups. But I always ask the caller a few questions before I tell him what we are doing. And one of the first statements I make is, "I want to be sure you keep your job; I don't want you to get fired." We both laugh and then the phone goes silent as the person on the other end realizes how serious I am.

FIRST QUESTIONS

Let's take a look at some of the key first questions every minister should ask before launching a small-group ministry.

"Are you in a small group?"

My first question to anyone calling about starting small groups is, "Are you in a small group?" This is a question our team asks every week in the halls of LifePoint or at our guest-services booth. It is one of the first questions the LifePoint Church office asks when a crisis hits a family. It is a question we ask at a ballgame, at the store, or at community events as we meet someone who attends LifePoint. And it is a question anyone considering small-group ministry must ask himself or herself.

The most common response I receive is, "No, we are just considering starting them at our church." This answer gives me a lot of insight into where we need to go in our discussion and the purpose of the call. *You can't take people where you are not.* The movement to a small-group ministry cannot be because another church has them. The opening statement should never be, "I heard about it at a conference" or "My pastor suggested starting small groups." (However, if you receive that last comment, you might want to get a small group started!)

Small groups are not a *program*. They may be called a process or a ministry, but should not be seen as a program. I become concerned about the future of small groups in a church when I hear them referred to as a program. The process to implement a program is not organic, not relational, and often includes no buy-in opportunities from the leadership.

You need to be *in* a small group in order to *start* small groups. You don't have a story unless you are in a group. Small-group ministry grows as much from the story than from a program implementation.

I was a minister of education for twenty years and only attended Sunday school class a few times a year. Most of my ministry I worked in Sunday school leadership and could not attend a class. And as I recall, most of my pastors were not in a Sunday school class unless they were teaching a pastor's class. We did not have the joy of being part of a group of individuals who studied God's Word together. But we did have a program that all our staff knew well, knew how to move people to, and knew the goal. For us the goal was to grow Sunday school by adding as many people to the classes as possible. Many of these people had community (relationships) with people outside the church or their class, but not a plan or culture in which to invite them. Bottom line: By being in a small group you have a better understanding of the culture, you are developing a story, and you are doing what you are going to ask others to do.

"Why small groups?" and "What do you hope to accomplish?"

Discovering what has brought the ministers or staff to the point of considering small groups helps in the design of next steps. LifePoint Church (then First Baptist Church, Smyrna) was experiencing a large amount of growth that led to space and serving issues. We did not have enough space for the adults who were already involved in Sunday school, much less space to start new units. We went from two worship services and two Sunday school hours, then to three of each. This brought issues with the preschool and children's ministries because they needed more people to serve. I often joked that our children's minister would cry while the adult staff celebrated when more families joined the church. Adult ministries might gain a person or two, but the children's division always gained three or four children for every family. Space was becoming a problem.

We were also learning that the Sunday school program was accomplishing the numbers growth but not necessarily the spiritual growth or community. We also noticed a key philosophic issue: Adult participants didn't have the opportunity to create the community and accountability necessary for discipleship in such large classes or in this academic-style learning environment. In other words, what we wanted to accomplish could not happen in our existing programs or space. What we hoped to accomplish—discussed in chapter 3—can be summed up in three words: discipleship, community, and service.

Take a look at the concerns your church may have, which the staff may be trying to solve by adding small groups; this will help keep the ministry pilot groups from being a failure. The answers to these two questions help you evaluate what you already have in place, guiding you through the issues and culture that already exist and clarifying the goal or objectives you wish to meet.

"Can this be accomplished in a current ministry?"

I was minister of education and administration of First Baptist Church, Smyrna from 1995 to 2000. In 2000 I went to work for LifeWay Christian Resources as a church consultant and leadership specialist in new believer follow-up. This job soon moved me to Kentucky. While in Kentucky I was introduced to Willow Creek Church and the many conferences they offer. My pastor at that time, Dr. Virgil Grant, took me on my first trip to Willow Creek where we participated in the small-group conference. I had only dabbled in small groups up to that point. Virgil helped me understand the culture needed for small-group ministry to succeed.

Then in 2005 First Baptist Church, Smyrna called me to return as adult small-groups pastor. I spent the summer of 2005 meeting with all the small-group leaders and teams, trying to understand the culture. As I met with each small-group leader, I heard stories of community, life transformation, and passion for others.

In the fall of 2005 our entire staff attended the annual Drive Conference at North Point Church in Atlanta. On our drive to Atlanta a lot of discussion took place about the future of small groups. I had been considering calling both Sunday school (which took place on-campus) and small groups (which took place off-campus) the combined title of "Life Groups." The staff received this idea as only a church staff can receive the new guy—with respect and quiet response so as not to offend or embarrass me.

At the conference, Andy Stanley took the stage to offer one of his thought-provoking and challenging messages. Our entire staff sat on the front row of the balcony while Stanley began to talk about change and calling things what they really are. Then he said it—the statement that caused the entire row of First Baptist Church staff to lean over, look at me, and, in unison, *laugh at me*. Stanley said, "Why in the church do we try to change something by just changing the name? If the program is not bringing the desired results, don't just put a new name on it!" We all knew immediately that our current Sunday school program could not produce the needed results we had been discussing, which were discipleship, community, and service.

I am happy to report that five years later many of our on-campus groups (formerly Sunday school classes) have made the journey in their classes from lecture-only to groups trying to accomplish discipleship, community, and service, as well as participating in celebration and development opportunities.

It is a common practice among church leadership to add something to an existing organization to fix the identified weaknesses. People in your church know if you have done the research on the current processes. They know when you are just trying to add a new program because you heard it at a conference. You must evaluate and discuss transitioning them or adding to them if you are attempting to fix a problem.

The definition of small groups is growing and changing and depends on your church's history and background. Therefore, you must define what you want to accomplish with small groups in order to position them correctly. Several churches I have worked with have called their on-campus, semester-based weekly discipleship ministry small groups. (This was based on the idea that the groups would not be larger than twelve participants.) The actual purpose for these type of groups was to work through and complete the study in six, eight, or thirteen weeks; then the group was finished. The next semester participants join a different short-term group based on the subject. These classes had nothing to do with community, but were based on the title or description of the study. However, as noted at the beginning of this chapter, small groups should not be defined by size, when they meet, what they produce, or what they study. Those things are not the description of small-group ministry as practiced at LifePoint.

I spent eight years perfecting the design, promotion, and implementation of this revolving study-group model. The result was many adults completing many studies but not having community with each other. Our research showed the same few adults were involved in the discipleship program each semester. We now refer to this as the merry-go-round effect, due to its cyclical nature of drawing the same adults semester after semester. We were led to try the small-group model because we determined that our current ministries could not accomplish the goals and objectives we desired.

"How does discipleship happen at your church?"

In 1998 First Baptist Church was one of the leading churches in the state for discipleship opportunities. The Sunday and Wednesday evening classes were titled University of Life and had over twenty class options each semester. This was the program responsible for discipleship. It was not the only place discipleship was happening, but this was the program that was focused on discipleship. After five years of offering University of Life, the leadership of First Baptist began to do research on the impact this college-style discipleship was having. To our surprise, University of Life was seeing the same 150 people rotating through classes (merry-go-round effect) semester after semester. Although Sunday morning attendance was more than a thousand, the adults who participated in University of Life were limited, due to lack of interest or they were already serving in other ministries at those same times.

As we considered the results of this research, small groups became more obvious as the answer for the next step on the journey. We defined discipleship for small groups in a way each person could measure his or her own progress; the small-group leader would have clear objectives for which to strive. We customized the *Spiritual Health Assessment and Spiritual Health Planner* from Saddleback Church[2] to meet our needs, which clarified the goals for discipleship, community, and service.

Discussing how a church wants to disciple people is a touchy subject. Many elements can influence discipleship. However, usually there is one division or part of a ministry that is focused on discipleship. Will it be mainly through the sermons, semester classes, or an organization that is organic and ongoing? Answering this question for your church may not be easy, but it is necessary. While we agree that all these elements play a part in the discipleship of adults, at LifePoint Church small groups have become the avenue for intentional discipleship.

"What do your pastor, staff, and/or leadership team think about small groups?"

Rick Warren has been very beneficial for many of us in the world of small groups. One of the greatest contributions to small-group ministry has been his constant mentioning of small group in his sermons. Andy Stanley has helped each of us as he tells stories about his small group in the middle of his sermons. Bill Hybels talks often about his sailing group, which he treats like a small group. John Piper has even been videotaped in his sermons passionately requesting everyone in his congregation to join a small group.

I realize that most of us will not have the opportunity to serve with such influential pastors. But you can spend time with your own pastor and staff and share your heart regarding small groups; if all else fails, send them links to Internet podcasts of the pastors mentioned above.

At a small group summit in 2010, author and speaker Lyman Coleman was asked whether a church could have a successful small-group ministry without the senior pastor's total support. He responded, "No, I have never seen a successful small-group ministry in a church unless the senior pastor is the champion of it."[3]

Getting direction and support from the pastor is crucial, vital, required, and necessary. Your pastor may not have attended the conference you did. He does not have the vision or the hours of research on the subject that you have. Take some time to evaluate and discuss current programming with your pastor and staff. Be realistic about expectations for these programs and ministries. With what you know and have heard, could small groups be a solution for the weaknesses identified in your church? What is the tone of the discussions with the pastor and staff? Having a team spirit in launching small groups will determine to what extent small groups are a success.

"What will be the expectations for or responsibility of church staff in small-group ministry?"

Will the staff of your church be expected or required to be in a small group? Will each staff member be required to lead an adult small group, no matter his or her ministry role?

I remember the day it happened. My pastor at LifePoint Church, Pat Hood, was sitting in his office working on his next sermon. The small office where he does his planning has a desk, bookshelves, and one chair for staff when they come in to chat. I sat down in that chair trying to get my thoughts in order before I blurted out a wrong statement. Pat usually types away as I talk, but this time he stopped and asked me, "What is it?" As he turned his chair toward me I blurted out, "Do you expect our staff to be in small groups?" I felt like a kid who had just told his dad he wrecked the car. I knew those words came out wrong. Pat is a quick thinker, a driven person who is passionate about seeing more and more people step across the line of faith and have their lives transformed. He ignored the inelegance with which I had phrased my question and responded by saying, "If we are going to see people grow in community and be discipled, if this is an important next step for people who attend our church, then yes, all of us have to be in a small group." Pat has three words with which he evaluates everyone we interview for a ministry staff position: character, competency, and chemistry.[4] He also shares two expectations for all staff: first, that you tithe; and second, that you create no surprises for him. For him to add small groups to the list of expectations for staff was a major win for the entire GroupLife division, and for me.

This became the guiding practice for LifePoint: The staff are expected to be in a small group. They do not have to lead a small group, but they have to be in one. There are a few reasons why this is so important. One was for adult community and accountability. It is easy to lead a ministry and not experience the community and ministry. As mentioned earlier, many pastors and staff are unable to attend Bible study classes due to their Sunday morning responsibilities. Many preschool and children's ministry workers are unable to have adult interaction about God's Word. Small groups provide the option for staff and leadership to be in a Bible study group at a time that works for them. Another reason for staff involvement in a small group is that it sets the example that small groups are important. This is not an optional event; it is where life happens and discipleship takes place.

The staff agreed on the guiding purpose for small groups found in Acts 2:42-47. Now we have a pastor and staff united around this verse and the three objectives of small-group ministry.

Church staffs have led some of the most successful launches of small-group ministry as they piloted the first small groups of their church. As you begin the small-group ministry movement, consider asking each staff person to pilot or start a small group. In addition, the minister of education or small-group point person may start a new small group focused on apprenticing several leaders at once, often called a "turbo group." Bill Donahue, formerly with Willow Creek Association in Chicago, initiated the idea of turbo groups. In his book *Leading Life-Changing Small Groups,* he defines a turbo group as "a turbocharged small group designed to intentionally develop and release leaders, thus starting several new groups at once as it births."[5]

This season of pilots generates stories and experiences to share with others and gives them a test field for the direction they want to take in small groups. By having staff involved in this early phase, the avenues for stories of life change and understanding the importance of small groups are multiplied.

"What is success for a small-group leader?"

My family has been involved in church all my life. When I was five years old I sat in our car with my mother as we watched my father and other men of First Baptist Church, Riverview, Michigan, raise the first wall of the new church building. Ever since that day my father and mother have been heavily involved in Sunday school, many times with my father as the teacher. All my life I have learned in Sunday school and about Sunday school. I spent twenty years learning and leading Sunday school ministries. Did you ever have the Sunday school bell in your church? You know, when the Sunday school hour has five minutes before conclusion, this bell rings. Then five minutes later it rings again, meaning time to go to worship. No one ever really knew who rang the bell or where the button was, but we all knew what it meant. The first bell signaled *hurry up and get finished with today's lesson.* The second bell meant *hurry up and pray so we can leave.* Now we all know that this is not actually the meaning of the bell, but for *this* child, teenager, and eventually adult, these were the thoughts that went through my head. One thing that became ingrained in me were the unwritten goals or measures of success for a Sunday school teacher: (1) Get through the material. (2) On time.

Ministry goals, objectives, or purposes for small groups are very important. More directly, what is success for a small-group leader and small-group ministry? Earlier we discussed the question "What do you want to accomplish in small-group ministry?" The success question takes this a step further for the small-group leader and your leadership team. Based on your discussion with your pastor and staff, how can you state the goal for a small-group leader more specifically? As much as we may wish to avoid using statistics or data to define success, at every staff meeting there is the discussion of numbers, attendance, receipts, baptisms, and so on. What will you measure, and how? What will be success for a small-group leader? These expectations for success must be in writing; they must be very clear and communicated often.

For the last several years, LifePoint has revolved around discipleship, community, and service as objectives for the small-group ministry. But this is just a general designation; the expectations are much clearer and fall under each of these objectives. To facilitate understanding, we have listed three specific activities that help the pastor, staff, small-group team, and small-group leader know what success looks and feels like.

The world of small groups is so organic that it may seem futile to even try to define success by objectives that are, dare I say, permanent. But having these expectations as a clear target is what distinguishes LifePoint Church from many other small-group ministries.

- **Discipleship**: We expect groups to fulfill this objective by conducting Bible study at least two times a month and praying for those far from Christ. They should encourage members of the small group to participate in corporate worship as well as have a daily quiet time (devotional life). They must constantly look to develop future leaders (apprentice).
- **Community**: The expectation is for small groups to have a party every month. Once a quarter we expect the party to focus on their friends who are far from Christ or to invite new people to the group. Leaders are to strive to develop community so the opportunity for transparency increases, which also increases accountability. We ask them to always seek to share the load of small group by letting people use their passion, gifts, and talents to serve the group.
- **Service**: We help define this objective with four areas for service to be lived out by the small group as a whole and each member individually. These are the church, community, each other, and around the world. Leaders should help members find a place to serve at church, while not diminishing the need and joy received from serving the community. Groups are expected

to have service projects in the community. Some of these projects are annual, while many result in monthly projects. LifePoint Church is a missional church that provides several opportunities to serve globally as well.

The clear communication of these expectations for a small-group leader is enhanced by the church culture. Prior to the launch of small groups, LifePoint Church had already been working to develop core values and expectations for the congregation. The core values (see appendix, page 169) drive our discussions and decisions; we communicate them through the bulletin, signage around the building, and in the Discover LifePoint class (see appendix), the required class for membership. But we did not stop there. To narrow the focus for the participants, we arrived at five characteristics we believe define a disciple (see appendix). These characteristics help us take the next step on the journey of being Christ-centered. There are many characteristics of a Christ follower, but we narrowed our list to these five to better focus on what we, as a church, could influence. The five expectations of LifePoint are worship, biblical community, service, influence, and generosity.

With our core values and expectations already determined, the objectives for small-group ministry became clear: discipleship, community, and service. Because we walked through this process, we saw a unity develop churchwide. Success for a small-group leader and the small-group ministry is to involve as many people as possible in these three objectives on a regular basis.

"How will we count attendance?"

Sometimes it is very difficult to meet on a weekly basis for Bible study because life responsibilities interfere. Traditional attendance processes will not always work for keeping records when life happens. How you talk about counting people in a small group and the way you speak toward attendance can greatly influence these ministry and community experiences.

Attendance counting continues to be one of our biggest ongoing discussions about small groups. Attendance is not one of the first questions to discuss, but be aware of underlying issues and ministry opportunities as you begin small-group ministry.

Every church can tell you how many people were in worship and Sunday school last week. They both meet on-campus and attendance is easily taken. However, small groups meet in the community whenever the group can get together, and many groups only meet specifically for a Bible study two times a month—so the traditional way of counting the impact the ministry is having cannot be used for this type of group. We have decided, and continue to educate our team, that attendance at a Bible study-specific meeting is not all we want to hear about. When a small group helps a neighbor in time of crisis, most of the people in the group participate. The socials or parties every month (one per quarter being specifically for our unchurched friends, in whom we have been investing and praying for daily) usually have conversations around what we have been dealing with and these also build community.

We have built such community in many small groups that you could call any member and he or she could tell you where each person in their small group is, and exactly what that person is dealing with or worrying about. Small groups are designed to be so intimate that people know about each other, all the time. We shifted our thinking about *attendance*; now we call it *involved*. (We tried the word *enrolled*, but that brought up another discussion about Sunday school. Sunday school classes do not count the total number enrolled, only those who are in attendance on that Sunday.) So *involved* is used; this is the number of people we can find, know something about, and are aware of their efforts to be a disciple—even if they missed last week's Bible study meeting.

Small-group ministry is organic. This means it is continually evolving into a new lifestyle. We are now adding to the attendance/

involvement record keeping by asking for groups to report all activity they do as a group. You may recognize this as "the story." We do not track attendance as much as we listen for the story. Monthly reports are run on all small groups. Through these communication reports, we can see who officially met and who did not. But in addition, we are asking for the story of life in the group.

The weekly online reporting system allows for comments and prayer requests. Using this tool is one way to share the story. Coaches are trained to listen for the story in all conversations and to avoid the "Why hasn't your group met?" or "I noticed you did not turn in attendance for your group" comments. (More about coaches in chapter 3.)

Small-group meeting is not always about studying the Bible; sometimes it is living out the Bible. When a crisis occurs, many people respond with the thought, *I don't have time to meet* or *Life is tough right now and I just can't meet with anyone.* In actuality, you do need to be around the people who are walking with you. You need to have time to process, to be comforted, to have a shoulder to cry on, to be around people who love you.

The small group offers help in hurting times. Meeting is not only about the material to be studied or about the required meetings per month, it is about giving people who are hurting time to talk about the difficult times in life. Dropping off food is a great blessing and necessity, but you can't hear the hurts of the person during a doorstep, casserole drop-off. Small groups allow people to be there for each other, allow opportunities—enough time together—for conversations to go beyond, "How are you doing?"

Many people who have sinned are embarrassed to attend small group or church, when what they really need to do is get back in the presence of God ASAP. Isolation is Satan's playground. When we have messed up or have a family crisis, we tend to want seclusion; but this only increases our loneliness and vulnerability to the Devil. Small group is a place of openness, forgiveness, comfort, and love.

For example, say a group member has a death in the family. You may call off the meeting because life is difficult right now and "they have a lot going on." They may feel like—or even specifically articulate—"the last thing I want to do is meet." Of course they are busy. Of course they don't want to meet. These responses further express why you have to spend time with them to help them process, to help them grieve, to have a small group around them that is like family. None of us needs to be alone (although we say we do) when times of sorrow or depression occur. We need God and we need people who represent God to be around us. While this time may not be counted as a meeting, it is a natural part of life as a growing Christ follower.

The attendance process does not have to be decided up front but will have to be discussed as the small-group ministry grows. This is not a battle to be won or lost in the early stages of small-group ministry. My grandfather taught me years ago, "A dog can whip a skunk, but it ain't worth it." Do not fight the battle concerning counting too early, but pray, study, and be prepared for this discussion when it arises.

"Where will groups meet?"

Another question that will be asked eventually is, "Where will the groups meet?" This subject will come up at least annually in a team meeting or discussion with a small-group leader. Where you meet is important. The relationships and casual atmosphere necessary for small groups to thrive cannot happen in an academic, institutional environment.

I was preparing the ice for the drinks at our every-other-week small-group meeting. As I walked back through the kitchen, I heard one of our small-group members, Jason, discussing lawn-care business with my teenage son. It was not long before Jason asked Graham to mow his yard for him. Then another small-group member, Wes, mentioned some opportunities for Graham to do lawn care and gutter cleaning with him.

My youngest son came through the living room a few minutes later wearing his baseball jersey. Another member of our small group stopped him to ask when he played his next game. They bragged on him for his athletic ability and promised to come see one of his games. They did attend a week later, making my son feel so important.

Each of our small groups is experiencing this family feel. We *do life* together. What one family is dealing with, the entire group is dealing with, from attending ball games to taking care of each other's children. Without the interaction made possible by meeting in people's homes, our children might not get this kind of treatment from Bible study members.

Where you meet is important. Being in someone's home, watching the kids run through the room, noticing the photos on the wall, getting "refrigerator rights"[6] are all crucial community-building experiences that cannot be encountered in a classroom on campus. "Refrigerator rights" describes the feeling that you can walk in someone else's house, open the fridge and help yourself—much like you feel at your mother's house. It is not about the fridge, of course, it is about the community and friendship and closeness you have with the owner. By meeting in homes, you get to experience a person and a family in its true, unfiltered life. You not only know where the refrigerator is, you can get what you need. You know the kids, how they interact, what they love, how to pray and care for them. You learn what is important to the family, what is sacred, and what is a no-no in their home. You have the opportunity to build community at a deep level. Meeting in homes increases community and accountability while building unity among families who participate in them.

The growth we have seen in community because of a smaller size group meeting in someone's home has shown us the importance of not meeting on-campus. Knowing what people value in their home, their decorating style, and the family life as the kids are allowed to be themselves in front of other adults is invaluable. For my family, when anyone from our small group sees one of my children, they have the right and permission to speak into his life—because we know them and we are family.

Where your groups meet can make a difference in the community people experience in small-group ministry.

SMALL-GROUP LEADER

Most of these questions will not affect a small-group leader because most of them should be settled before groups are started churchwide. However, small-group leaders do need to be aware of the answers to these questions. As they teach, lead, and facilitate the groups, knowing and understanding the church objectives will be important. These key questions serve as the foundation of the leader's purpose and supplies him or her with parameters in which to lead. Knowing that all of the staff are expected to be in a group helps leaders know this is important. Discipleship is what the leader strives for not only in his own life but also in each life that he is allowed to lead. The answers to these key questions gives leaders guidance for what and how to accomplish this discipleship. The objectives serve as a continual reminder of the goal for the small group and its leader. It is more than just meeting and counting attendance each week. The story that God is revealing in each person's life drives leaders to lead, to listen, to share, and to facilitate community.

Most of my own group has memorized Acts 2:42-47, which serves as our guiding scripture for the group. The passage describes the reasons we eat together at each meeting and rotate homes as much as possible as we open the Bible and discover the next truth God has for us on our journey.

Each week I have the privilege of hearing stories of people experiencing spiritual growth. I watch for life-changing comments, prayer requests, or offers to serve from group members. Here are some guiding questions that run through my mind about each individual in my group: Do I know where Bobby is right now? What is he dealing with, and how can I pray for him? What do we need to study next to help each other be more like Christ and experience discipleship, community, and service? Who can I invest a little more time in so he can be an apprentice to start another group or take over this group as I step out and lead another group?

Maybe these questions can help guide your thoughts about your group. Consider where God is leading you next and how you can help someone go with you.

A Church Story

When we met with Eddie in the summer, we were anticipating starting off-campus groups at our central campus only. When everything settled in the late fall, we had eighty-three off-campus groups and forty on-campus groups. Almost immediately our adult attendance doubled from what it had been with on-campus groups only.

Following the six-week commitment, we asked groups if they wanted to continue meeting. Almost 90 percent of our groups decided to keep going. We can take no credit for what God is doing here because we don't have any answers. All we know is that we listened and implemented a strategy we felt had the best potential for success. God blessed the efforts and we have seen unprecedented attendance and excitement throughout every area of our church.

— Terry Hadaway, Longhollow Baptist Church, Hendersonville, Tennessee

FIVE PRACTICAL STEPS FOR . . .

Your Ministry:

1. Talk with your pastor and staff about the goals of your discipleship and community ministry. Are they being met?
2. What are the objectives of your church's discipleship process?
3. Do the leaders in your biblical community division know the

objectives of the ministry? How can you promote them better?

4. Pick three of the "First Questions" from this chapter and discuss them with a trusted friend. Are these things you can discuss with your pastor and staff?

5. Make a list of five people who could become new small-group leaders and pray for them daily, by name, for three months.

Your Small Group:

1. What are the objectives for your small-group?

2. Identify an apprentice in your group and spend time this week discussing the goals and objectives of your small group with him or her.

3. Next group meeting, take time to have everyone write the goals for your group. This may be a part of the group's covenant (list of agreements).

4. Enlist someone from the group to be in charge of sharing stories from your group with the church. Each time you do something (Bible study, party, event) send an e-mail to the church, letting them know your group's life story.

5. Contact your church's small-group point person and discuss what you are doing to better communicate and accomplish the objectives. This is a good time to bring up any questions that have arisen too.

PRAGMATIC STRATEGY (ORGANIZATION)

When I was a teenager I worked at a department store. The manager, W. P. Kelly, educated me on an important rule: "Lack of communication causes wars. Whether it is between your mother and father, husband and wife, president and congressman, or boss and employee. Matters not, lack of communication causes wars." I have never forgotten his coaching, and I always communicate and try to be as clear as possible. In this chapter, I'll try to overcommunicate the importance of organization. The details that follow are written from information gained in conferences, books, phone calls, and experiences. These experiences have come from our GroupLife ministry as well as other churches' successes and failures. You'll see that this chapter is about communication as much as it is about strategy and organization. What you design from the information in this chapter will be vital—and how you communicate it just as important!

The small-group ministry has the potential to become multifaceted and grow rapidly, because when your church leaders and participants catch the vision, many lives will be affected and people will want to be on board. You will need to design a strategy and organization to enlist, develop, and multiply leaders to handle the influx, as well as carry out your assimilation process. This chapter will walk you through the strategy and organization. (The next chapter will focus on assimilation.)

How you keep all this working from week to week — keeping leaders focused on the vision yet ministering to others—requires a strategy, a practical one that people can easily follow. Your organizational design will greatly influence how large and how fast the small-group ministry can grow, and how well leaders and members understand the objectives and goals. Nehemiah faced an organizational situation when rebuilding the wall. It all began with these few words:

> Then I said to them, "You see the trouble we are in, how Jerusalem lies in ruins with its gates burned. Come, let us build the wall of Jerusalem, that we may no longer suffer derision." And I told them of the hand of my God that had been upon me for good, and also of the words that the king had spoken to me. And they said, "Let us rise up and build." So they strengthened their hands for the good work. (Nehemiah 2:17-18)

Moses also had need of organization when he sat as judge for the people, trying to do it all alone. It took a visit from his father-in-law, though, for him to understand:

> Moses went out to meet his father-in-law and bowed down and kissed him. And they asked each other of their welfare and went into the tent. . . . Jethro said, "Blessed be the LORD, who has delivered you out of the hand of the Egyptians. . . . Now I know that the LORD is greater than all gods. . . ."
>
> The next day Moses sat to judge the people, and the people stood around Moses from morning till evening. When Moses' father-in-law saw all that he was doing for the people, he said, "What is this that you are doing for the people? Why do you sit alone, and all the people stand around . . . ?" And Moses said to his father-in-law, "Because the people come to me to inquire of God; when they have a dispute, they come to me and I decide between one person and another, and I make them know the statutes of God and his laws." Moses' father-in-law said to him, "What you are doing is not good. You and the people with you will certainly wear

yourselves out, for the thing is too heavy for you. You are not able to do it alone. Now obey my voice; I will give you advice, and God be with you! You shall represent the people before God and bring their cases to God, and you shall warn them about the statutes and the laws, and make them know the way in which they must walk and what they must do. Moreover, look for able men from all the people, men who fear God, who are trustworthy and hate a bribe, and place such men over the people as chiefs of thousands, of hundreds, of fifties, and of tens. And let them judge the people at all times. Every great matter they shall bring to you, but any small matter they shall decide themselves. So it will be easier for you, and they will bear the burden with you. If you do this, God will direct you, you will be able to endure, and all this people also will go to their place in peace."

So Moses listened to the voice of his father-in-law and did all that he had said. (Exodus 18:7-24)

It took someone with more experience, someone standing on the outside looking in, to see that Moses was working himself to death — that he needed a better strategy to accomplish everything that needed to be done for the people under his care.

What kind of organization have you designed to help people move closer to being more like Christ? What strategy are you considering? What practical steps can you put in place to allow this ministry to grow?

A friend of mine, Rich Smith, researched to discover which type of small-group model and strategy would meet his church's needs. Perhaps his summary will help you as you seek the model that works best for your situation:

In my doctoral studies, I recently engaged in a project that required me to research the various different types of small group models. . . .

As I conducted my research I quickly found there existed a number of different small group models for various types, sizes, and worship styles of congregations. The G-12 model . . . focused on the importance of each small group, consisting of twelve people who targeted raising up twelve new leaders, in order to complete a G-12 cycle. Needless to say, [this] model required ambitious leaders to achieve such a high goal. . . .

The next model I discovered was the meta-church model, which . . . simply meant that as congregations grew larger in corporate size, they would continue to grow smaller through networks of small groups.

Free market groups . . . centered on various people's shared interest on things outside of the church, including sports and hobbies . . . these groups typically lasted for a semester throughout a school or church year. . . .

Other small group models that I researched focused on strategic discipleship, as well as support groups that helped both believers and the unchurched to overcome similar and difficult life circumstances, such as divorce. . . .

As I narrowed my research, I directed my . . . attention to missional or evangelistic small groups. These groups placed their focal point within the community and more specifically within neighborhoods and residential areas of our congregation's members. . . .

Among the various small group models that I studied, they all shared a couple of affinities. One, they all placed a high priority on reproducing leaders as well as reproducing groups. Second, they took similar, but somewhat different, approaches on launching their small groups, as well as training their first-generation leaders.

Finally, at the lowest common denominator for all of these various small group models, as well as leadership training processes, they find their roots . . . in an environment of safe relationships, better known as community.[1]

THE PILOTS MULTIPLY

The pilot stage is nearing completion and the launch is just a few months away. This is the time to draw up an initial strategy for multiplying leaders and enlarging the organization. Each of the pilots will have potential small-group leaders or apprentices they have been training. Meet with these potential leaders and share the vision with them. They not only need to hear from you, but you need to allow them to speak into the strategy for the next few months. This will give them ownership and help you see this ministry from a different perspective. As you create the strategy for the next steps, bear in mind it should not be written in stone because small-group ministry is organic; the strategy will evolve as you learn, grow, and experience all that God has for you and your church.

Now is the time to identify one or two people who have been through the pilot project and understand the vision for small groups. They have been impacted by what they have experienced and are anxious for others to experience this as well. Let them walk beside you in your leadership of small-group ministry. Train them on the vision, strategy, issues, and processes of small groups at your church. Take them to conferences, buy them books, and share blogs and websites with them for their continued development; communicate with them often. These are the people who could be vital to the small-group ministry in the near future.

CLEAR OBJECTIVES

By now you should be seeing a picture of what small groups should be, what they are to accomplish, and their place in the ministry of your church. Having clear objectives for the small-group ministry so the leader, the participant, the coaches, the staff, and the pastor can understand, process, and discuss will be important. These objectives can be tweaked and more narrowly defined as the ministry grows.

In the 1990s, pastor and author Rick Warren of Saddleback Church began a movement toward establishing the five purposes of the church as guiding objectives. These five purposes—worship, ministry, evangelism, fellowship, and discipleship—are Bible-based purposes. Each of Saddleback's small groups is to adopt them and have people identified within the group to champion each one.[2] Another author, speaker, and small-groups pastor, Bill Search of Southeast Christian Church in Louisville, Kentucky, has written a book *Simple Small Groups* in which he not only shares his story but also has clearly defined the objectives for his small-group ministry. Bill's objectives are to connect, change, and cultivate.[3] Pastor Virgil Grant of Eastside Church in Richmond, Kentucky, has mapped out his church's small-group objectives as belong, become, bless.[4] And you have already read about LifePoint's small-group objectives: discipleship, community, and service.

Any of these might work for your church, but I encourage you to think through the direction of small-group ministry for your church. Make it your own, specific to the direction of your ministry. These objectives need to represent your church's language, DNA, and culture. They need to point people toward the biblical principles for which your small-group ministry is being designed.

Another guiding article you will want to design and have in place as the ministry launches is a small-group covenant, sometimes called a list of agreements or group guidelines. The covenant will help communicate the objectives of small group to every participant. A covenant levels the playing field, so every leader and member knows what is expected.

For LifePoint Church, the covenant evolved over the first few years of small-group ministry implementation. When we started, most of the guidance for small-group ministry and covenant wording came from books we had read or conferences we had attended. Some of the groups even made up their own covenant. Years later we adapted the information we had accumulated into a covenant written specifically for LifePoint Church, using common language and the objectives LifePoint's small-group ministry already had in place (see appendix for sample covenant).

A covenant is very important as the ministry grows. Now that we have been in small-group ministry for several years we understand even more the importance of the covenant. We estimate that 80 percent of the problems that arise in small groups could have been addressed, maybe even avoided, if the group had discussed the covenant early in its life. Having clear objectives and a small-group covenant will be one more way of communicating the focus of small groups.

Mission by the Pool

Not often do we get the opportunity to serve others in a way that is just "absolute silly fun," but this was one of those times! The Laminin small group partnered with the management at a local apartment complex to assist them with their annual summer pool party. Our mission was to establish relationships, with the hope of planting seeds for small-group studies among the tenants – and just have good fun with a positive vibe!

Our group helped plan and set up the event, working hand-in-hand with property management and the maintenance crew on the day of the event. Then we had fun at the pool, throwing the Frisbee, participating in the hula hoop contest, and serving hotdogs, chips, drinks, and popcorn. Todd brought his cotton candy machine and donated all the ingredients, and we also provided a jumper on the tennis courts for the children, which they thoroughly enjoyed.

The Laminin Group T-shirts we were wearing made for the perfect icebreaker; they allowed us to share how Christ holds us together. We explained the benefit of being involved in a small group for weekly Bible study, being an encouragement to one another through prayer support, and holding one another accountable as Christ follow-ers. Stories were shared from those who were broken and searching for God. As a group we learned that even in the midst of playful laughter, there are hurts from things unseen and people who are crying out for someone to care. It was an awesome day for us to care for those folks and share the good news that there is hope in Jesus Christ. Our group's mission statement proved to be real that day: "We are held together by Christ for His purpose."

— Dennis C.

LEADER QUALIFICATIONS AND APPRENTICING

As your ministry grows from the first pilot group to multiple groups, clarifying the qualification for a small-group leader is necessary. Leaders represent not only Christ but also the church and must come under the direction of the church. Let the pilot leaders help write a list of qualifications for the small-group ministry. Review your current list of qualifications for other ministries of your church. Out of this list and your goals for small groups, create a list especially for small-group leaders. This is LifePoint's list for small-group leader qualifications:

- Confess that Jesus Christ is your forgiver, leader, Lord and Savior, and have been baptized.
- Be an active member of LifePoint Church.
- Regard the Bible as the God-spoken authoritative guide in your life and faith.
- Hold to the vision and core values of LifePoint Church.
- Agree to come into the LifePoint GroupLife Ministry leadership structure.

One of the most important discussions to have with small-group leaders early in the group's life is about apprenticing. Apprenticing is one of the keys to continued small-group growth. Let me go ahead and say it — not all small groups or small-group leaders will have an apprentice. Not all small groups will multiply in a timely manner; they might not ever multiply. This is not necessarily the desired outcome, but it is reality. Nevertheless, it is important to talk often about apprenticing as a goal, for without that, groups may never catch the vision to reach or connect to others. Everyone has neighbors, coworkers, or other church attendees they know who would like to or need to connect. Without a plan and continued encouragement to launch a group with an apprentice, these people may never have the chance to join a small group.

Apprenticing is hindered by a common fear from leaders, often referred to as "splitting my group." After twenty-four years in ministry, education ministry–focused, I have only tried to split two classes. Both were obedient attempts in the nature of what I had been taught. Both caused me much heartburn, lost friendships, sleepless nights, and, in the end, brought no long-term additional classes.

Now the communication has changed. Each new small-group leader is asked and assisted with the enlistment of an apprentice from the very start of the group. We ask small groups to try to send out an apprentice in six, twelve, or eighteen months after the start of their group; Barna research relates that after eighteen months a group becomes closed.[5] "Closed" refers here to inwardly focused — groups who intentionally decide to not add people to the group so that they can go deeper in accountability or Bible study. In other cases these classes or groups become closed unintentionally because the members are so focused on each other that it is difficult, if not impossible, for new people to join the group. This closed mentality will not only limit growth but will often lead to destruction of the group. Small groups are designed for spiritual growth and influence in the lives close to them. An apprentice plan helps groups keep part of their focus on others and the growth of God's kingdom.

We promote sending out an apprentice a minimum of two times a year. Each winter and fall, LifePoint conducts churchwide campaigns around a sermon series and small-group study. This is a time we communicate about joining a small group. In conjunction with the churchwide study in the spring, we usually see multiple apprenticeships in a group. Last fall, a fairly new small-group leader challenged his group to reach out to their friends and neighbors to start a new, temporary small group for six weeks. Three of the five couples took the challenge and invited people to their house for the six weeks. Four months later, all four groups were still meeting and growing. They began to practice the discipleship, community, and service objectives of small groups. With an average of ten adults per small group, this equaled forty people in Bible study, compared to ten in the original group just a few months earlier.

Again, apprenticing will not always happen in a group. Rarely have we seen it happen as greatly as in this group's life, but keeping it as a foundational element in your ministry will help guide people into the future.

ENLISTING LEADERS

Where do we find more leaders? First, in the pilot groups you will have people who catch the vision and know of family members, friends, coworkers, and neighbors who need to experience life in a small group.

Turbo groups,[6] mentioned in the previous chapter, are also a great way to quickly develop more leaders and coleaders who can start groups and enlist apprentices immediately. When your organizational team grows, allow these folks to speak vision and share stories about apprenticing and starting other groups. This will help inspire more people to envision themselves leading a group.

The best marketing tool is still word of mouth. When Christ impacts people's lives through a small group, they begin to tell others. You can help them talk about their experiences—and start new groups. There is always the added bonus of information from the stage. When your pastor can talk about his *own* group—not just mention small groups—people will be interested. Look for opportunities to have people reveal their stories in short video clips, live on stage, or inside a sermon or announcements. Telling the stories of how small groups have helped change people's lives is the best communication you can have to draw out more leaders.

ASSIMILATION

Being a Christ follower is all about relationships—a relationship with Jesus Christ and a relationship with people. It is through relationships we enjoy life, we share life, and we experience life. Because of or through a relationship we hear about Christ, we inquire about Christ, and he reveals himself to us. Levi's story in Luke 5 is an inspiration to us all: "And leaving everything, [Jesus] rose and followed him. And Levi made him a great feast in his house, and there was a large company of tax collectors and others reclining at table with them" (verses 28-29).

With all the social media today—Facebook, MySpace, Twitter, and so on—we are able to know a lot about people and they are able to know a lot about us. Sometimes these "friends" are people who do not know us and people we do not truly know. The jury is still out on how true a connection and relationship can happen via these social media. Transparency is growing through these connections, but it's still limited. But true connection and foundational relationships are not as common as they were twenty-five years ago. People are mobile, programmed, scheduled, and focused on self—maybe too focused on work, family, and money. Christianity is not a lone religion; it is a living relationship. As Christ transforms our lives, it shows—and people are drawn to him. We have the opportunity to constantly communicate the stories of life change. Through sharing stories, the opportunity for assimilation will grow.

We will discuss assimilation in detail in chapter 4. This is the next step in the process of multiplying your small-group ministry.

COACHES

LifePoint's practical strategy for coaching takes into account the relational part of small-group ministry. We started with a few groups coached by one person, the small-group pastor. As the interest in small groups grew, the organization had to grow. Trios of small-group leaders were teamed together for support, direction, and ministry. They met monthly to pray, share, and to discuss small-group ministry. As the ministry grew, more communication was necessary to hear the stories about what God was doing and to keep other groups and leadership informed. Coaching gave us more opportunity to communicate these stories.

There are many views on how to lead, guide, or coach small-group leaders. You will have to adapt parts of all of them before you find what is right for your situation. Don't miss the role of relationship in coaching. Greg Bowman, coauthor of *Coaching Life-Changing Small Group Leaders*, guides coaches "to invest 90 percent of their energy in shepherding and listening to the needs of the leader and 10 percent in vision casting and leading them. Over time, weeks or maybe months, that ratio can begin to shift. But the shepherding gift never goes away. And at critical junctures in the leader's life, shepherding will take prominence over the leadership gift in the relationship."[7]

We define the three categories of coaching as shepherding, multiplying, and managing. We enlist coaches based on experience and fruit of their service as a small-group leader. Then we help them determine whether their natural tendency is more shepherding, multiplying, or managing. Shepherds will love, care for, and walk with their small-group leaders, providing guidance and welfare to them. Multiplying coaches will lean toward the growth of the ministry and be passionate about the unconnected or unchurched. The managing coach will work with their leaders to keep the records while adhering to the processes. You may need to have a combination of the three, depending on your church size and needs for growth and care. We have all three categories represented on LifePoint's coaching team.

Developing coaches has been vital to the continued growth, health, and retention of small groups. People's lives are impacted daily as they are involved in their own small group. Life brings the ups and downs of emotion, finances, family, job stress, and so forth. Coaches play an important role in helping small-group leaders handle the pressure of dealing with these issues in their groups. How you train and develop coaches will depend on the particular coach. Having a clear set of goals and multiple ways of accomplishing them will be very helpful. Coaches can help keep the groups focused on the objectives and increase the dissemination of the stories of small group.

Coaching has evolved over the years of small-group ministry at LifePoint Church. We are seeing transformation take place in the organic relationships that are being developed in our coaching structure. We have placed the emphasis for coaches on ministry and shepherding, rather than attendance reports. That said, attendance reports are important because they show signs of issues in a group. Your focus may be on tracking attendance or organization if your experience is from the management world like mine. My business degree creeps into ministry on a daily basis, but I have to allow my baseball-coaching career to impact my thinking as much if not more than my BBA. Management is useful. It gives reports and numbers that I use weekly. However, coaching keeps the focus on people.

One way we have helped coaches focus on ministry and story discovery is creating our slogan, "Two minutes a day and pray on the way." This is a challenge for every coach to call a small-group leader on the way home from work for a two-minute conversation. The relationship between the coach and the small-group leader grows naturally through conversation. The coach might learn what issues the small group is dealing with and how to pray for the group. The coach also is giving the opportunity for the leader to ask questions and get advice on leading the group.

The slogan also reminds coaches to pray for one of their leaders every day on the way to work. This keeps the leaders on the coach's mind all day and it demonstrates care for the leaders.

I have to admit in our first week of practicing this slogan, the issues were heavier than we had anticipated and two minutes turned into twenty minutes for a couple of our coaches. When one coach called me to complain about his extended conversation, my not-so-sympathetic response was, "Well, if it were not for the two minutes a day, you would not have known about these issues until it was too late. This way we get the opportunity to have an impact where leaders need help." The coach laughed and agreed it was a valuable conversation.

Another practice we are using is called the Four P's. Saddleback's Steve Gladen wrote these to help his coaches to classify each of their small-group leaders into one of four categories; this in turn helps them make more productive use of their time and effort. To coach a small-group leader is to walk in his life as a mentor, guide, and a person who shares his joys and pains.

- **Personal**: Small-group leaders in this category need their coach to chat, share a cup of coffee, and spend time talking about joys and hurts almost on a daily basis.
- **Priority**: Small-group leaders in this category may be new group leaders and young in their leadership experience. These are the leaders who are on the top of the coach's list for prayer, to contact often, and suggest resources or connect them with other small-group leaders who can mentor and guide. These may be the leaders who have urgent issues in the life of their group.
- **Phone**: You don't have to constantly encourage this level of leaders to communicate with you. They lead and communicate with you and others often, sharing needs and telling the

small-group story. Their leadership can be discovered, guided, and prayed for by an occasional phone call.

- **Persistent**: These are leaders who are aloof and adapt to things later or very hesitantly. The relationship must be constantly managed so that the leader begins to understand the vision, purpose, and the necessity to communicate and share. Coaches need to be there for these leaders by being persistent in their calls, cards, prayers, and visits.

Coaching small-group leaders is very important to the continued ministry and growth of small groups. How you decide to implement coaching will depend on the number of groups and growth of the church. It will also be determined by the infrastructure you put in place. Adapt what you learn from various approaches into an organized system that can grow and change as needed.

As our small-group ministry grew, we realized that the infrastructure had to change. Coaches were increasing in number and communication was more scattered; it was difficult to know all the small-group stories. Up to this point, coaches were (and still are) volunteers, but we had grown to the point that we needed more organization. We began to employ top-level coaches on a part-time basis as coordinators. We determined a ratio of one to five for coaches to small-group leaders and use the same ratio for coordinators to coaches. This allows more people to be involved in shepherding, multiplying, and managing small groups.

The coordinators are asked to be entrepreneurial in their leadership to keep organization healthy and multiplying. The ideal goal is for each coordinator to direct and build relationship with five coaches to accomplish discipleship, community, and service. They talk often and meet monthly with their coaches, who guide five small groups each. Coordinators also help lead the annual training events and quarterly small-group luncheons. Success for a coordinator is to know his coaches and small-group leaders by name, as well as each group's level of involvement in the three objectives. This new level of coaching has developed into a small-group leadership team who also help guide the direction of the ministry. But you can develop a small-group leadership team in your church without having to employ more people. Prayerfully ask the high-level volunteers to come alongside you and speak into the ministry.

BASIC PRINCIPLES

As the small-group ministry moves from pilots to a more formalized church organization (with objectives, qualifications, and coaches), basic principles by which the ministry lives and operates must be developed.

When I was growing up, our family had basic principles that it behooved you to follow. You never came to the dinner table without a shirt on, no matter how hot it was. You always offered visitors something to drink. We didn't mow the grass on Sunday, for that is the day of rest. You always said thank you. You never put your shoes on the kitchen counter, even if you were cleaning or shining them. You didn't talk back to your mother (took a few years for me to really understand this one). And I will say that conflicts or issues arose in our family when someone tried to live outside these basic principles.

I have come to view the small-group world in much the same fashion as a family, with basic principles by which to live. We help keep these basic principles in front of small-group leaders and members through the covenant, small-group website Groupleader.org, blogs, e-mails, quarterly luncheons for small-group leaders, and the quarterly small-group leadership team retreat.

Here are a few of the principles we stress at LifePoint.

Share the Load

Sharing the load[8] of small group is a *must*! By letting people serve in their passion, you are giving them responsibility in an area they are designed for and in which they may love to serve. With that responsibility comes ownership; they will want to make the meeting a success. My first few months as a small-group pastor, I interviewed every small-group leader of the church. In one interview a small-group leader told me he and his wife were burned out on leading small group. As I probed further it became obvious that he had never practiced the share-the-load principle. He said, "Every week my wife cooks supper for our group while I am cleaning the house and rearranging our living room so it will hold all of our group. Then she has to go pick up the babysitter before everyone arrives. By the time we finish the study and clean up the kitchen, it is time for my wife to pay the babysitter and take her home. Small group is killing my marriage and costing my family too much money."

I hope you can see several areas in which to share the load in this story. Some of the areas to share include child care, food, location, socials or parties, study choices, apprenticing, and/or leading. Discover every group member's passion or interest or hobby and let them own a part of the group. It could keep you from burnout. (There is more on this subject in chapter 5.)

Quarterly Parties

Evangelism happens through relationships more than any other approach. Every summer we encourage people to get out of their houses, walk their neighborhoods and meet people, and watch for God at work. The small groups are expected to have parties once a quarter and invite these new friends. People want to know about you before they make such a radical decision to attend church with you or step across the line of faith. Every month in our Discover LifePoint discovery class for those considering joining the church, we ask, "How did you find this church?"

Attendees usually have one of three answers: they viewed LifePoint's website; they drove by the "big building"; or—the number one answer—a friend, coworker, or relative invited them. Having a basic principle of quarterly parties to invite new people has helped to build a lot of relationships with those far from Christ. This in turn leads to relationships that can help draw people to Christ.

Curriculum Guide

A curriculum guide is a list of resources the GroupLife division has reviewed and approved for use in any small group. The basic principle is that group leaders should not stress over finding resources to use, but choose from resources that will help grow their group in the areas in which they struggle (see chapter 6 for more information on the curriculum guide).

Accountability

Small group will not be all it can be in your life without the desire to grow and be transparent and transformed. The accountability that can help lead to this transformation is a basic principle of small groups. You do not start with accountability; it is something that develops out of relationships, letting others walk in your life as you walk in theirs. Small-group leaders have learned that meeting in homes, eating together, and having time to talk before and after the Bible study is vital to building accountability.

Prayer

You may be surprised that this is listed as a basic principle for small groups. However, in my experience, the longer we are involved in church, church activities, and as a Christ follower, the less prayer seems to be a priority. But when the focus is on praying for each group member by name, daily, for a period of time, stories of God's activity just naturally bubble up and are shared. Throughout the year we suggest a three-month prayer rally to help focus a group, the leader, or the church prayer life—and then we watch for God to work.

Record Keeping

As mentioned previously, if your church has had on-campus Sunday school, a lot of discussion will happen around attendance. Record keeping is never easy and not a lot of fun to talk about. Letting you know who attended group last night is not something a leader wakes up and thinks about. Small-group leaders do not understand the importance of record keeping or they don't have time to process yesterday's events because today's events are approaching so rapidly. Yet keeping track is important for observing the health and growth of the people and ministry. Sometimes people will take offense to all the tracking, saying, "It is all about the numbers." And they're not off base: The focus should not be about the numbers for a Monday morning meeting; the focus should be on people and their lives being transformed. But one way we do that is keeping records. There are many software companies that can help with this, making the attendance and group information almost automatic. The difficulty comes more in the communication than in the process.

Additionally, to place attention on communication, we have changed the title of the attendance-reporting process to the Communication Report. Church Teams, a Web-based small-group software company[9] we use, has an automatic e-mailing system that sends a communication report request on the day after your meeting to the person who is sharing the load of the group by taking on the responsibility of completing the report. The report asks several questions about the group, including prayer requests, what the group is studying, and who was in attendance. Research how you want to keep records of attendance and information on groups. Communicate often the need to share stories.

TOP TEN QUESTIONS

In *Destination Community*, Rick Howerton has developed the top ten questions most often asked about participation in small groups.[10] We answered these questions for our church, and then put them on our website and in handouts. These ten questions gave us an avenue to communicate our strategy and organization to all interested people. Answering these questions has helped many small-group leaders know the way to respond to the practical issues people have about small groups. These are the top ten questions people ask about small groups, with answers specific to LifePoint Church.

1. How much of my time is this going to take?

The small-group Bible study meetings are usually a couple of hours long, meeting a minimum of two times a month. One hour for snacking, eating, and hanging out, another hour for Bible study. However, many small-group members begin to do life together, eating out, playing golf, boating, and even taking vacations together. The community that is built in a small group can be life changing. Most groups also have a monthly party and/or monthly or quarterly service project in which they serve.

2. What are we going to do with our children during small group?

The first hour of the meeting, the children hang out with the entire group. During Bible study, groups have various solutions they develop themselves, such as hire a babysitter (see babysitting ideas in chapter 5) for the group, have another home near the host home with a parent keeping them, or adults rotate keeping the kids in a another room in the house.

3. Will there be homework? If so, how much?

Most small groups do not have homework in a book. There may be daily devotionals that are suggested or weekly considerations to which you need to compare your life. Sometimes groups will read a book together, then meet to discuss it.

4. Am I going to have to talk or can I just sit and listen during meetings?

Small group is like family — sometimes you talk, sometimes you listen. No one is forced to talk or to lead the group. We all move at a different pace and you are allowed to do just that.

5. Will I have to pray out loud?

No. Again, you are allowed to move and grow at your own pace. If the time comes in your life that you feel you want to voice a prayer request, that will be well received. If the time comes you would like to lead in prayer, that will also be well received.

6. Who else is going to be in the group?

In the beginning, small groups are usually formed by the leader inviting friends, neighbors, or acquaintances to a cookout or social; there the host will announce and invite people to help start a small group. Another way we utilize for the formation of small groups is our church-wide GroupLink (for more on GroupLink see chapter 4). During the GroupLink promotion, you can connect with other adults and form a small group; you agree to try the small group for six weeks. At the end of the six weeks, each person can choose to continue with the group or not. This allows you a definite time to try a small group, but also have the assurance that there is a way out of this group if it does not work for you.

7. How much do I have to know about the Bible?

None. Small group is about learning the Bible, not debating it or being tested on it. During churchwide campaigns the sermons, worship songs, small-group studies, and daily devotionals are on the same subject and scripture. This is where we have experienced the most discipleship and most understanding of Bible truths, and is one reason you would want to be in a small group.

8. How many weeks or months is this group going to last?

Small group is like family, some of them last for years and others multiply and start new groups in twelve to eighteen months. We do ask that an apprentice be enlisted from the start so there is a plan to let others experience community in a small group as your group sends out the apprentice family at some point.

9. If I don't like it, can I leave without people being mad at me?

Yes, but most people build such community that they do not want to stop being part of the small group.

10. What are we going to be doing during the meetings?

Most meetings last a couple of hours. There is an hour for social, fellowship, eating, and building community, then another hour of Bible study, during which the group discusses and learns the material and scripture. There is always time for prayer and sharing of life issues, so people can help each other walk through life and not be alone. Basic principles are vital to the small-group ministry. Continued communication of the foundational elements will increase the understanding and life of the small-group ministry.

It looks like a lot of work, doesn't it? It is. But having a pragmatic strategy in place—a covenant, a plan for creating more leaders, and basic rules for groups to abide by—will save time and effort (and possibly blood, sweat, and tears) on the back end, when your program is up and running.

FIVE PRACTICAL STEPS FOR . . .

Small-Group Point Person:

1. How many of your pilot groups can become ongoing small groups? Make plans to meet with those leaders individually and discuss apprenticing.
2. Who are the potential small-group leaders and small-group coaches you have identified?
3. Of your current small-group leaders, can you assign each of them to one of the four P's?
4. Write how you will answer the small-group record-keeping question. It helps to clarify your thoughts.
5. Take a few days and think through the top ten questions about small groups and draft answers for your church, whether or not you have a program in place.

Your Small Group:

1. Do you know your church's small-group goals or objectives? How well do the people in your small group know them?
2. When was the last time you met with your coach? Were you transparent about your small group?
3. Review the basic principles established by your small-group pastor. Which ones are you practicing? Which one or two do you need to start practicing?
4. Who is keeping your small-group records (attendance)? Is this person sharing the story of the group often?
5. Who are you investing in as an apprentice? When will he be ready to start his own group?

ADAPT, DON'T ADOPT (ASSIMILATION)

A major part of church and small-group growth is assimilating the people God is sending to your church. *Assimilation* is the process of connecting people to the church—and to church programs or service opportunities. It's not always easy—especially in a larger church, where people can come and go and fail to be noticed—because successful assimilation is led by relationships. And the larger the church, the more important the relational focus of the assimilation process must be.

ONE SUCCESS STORY

Stevie and Hugo visited LifePoint on a Sunday morning in the early fall. They had recently gotten married and were seeking God. Stevie wondered if the church would actually accept their blended family and culture: Hugo was from Mexico and Stevie was from the United States. Stevie had done some research and was very interested in what the church had to offer her children and her new marriage. During the service, they heard an announcement about a GroupLink[1] event that was taking place that evening, which would help them connect to a small group. It sounded like everyone was supposed to be in a small group and seemed very important. Stevie and Hugo went home and discussed whether or not they should attend the event.

They did. As they entered the hallway a man named Billy greeted them and was very friendly and helpful. He helped them with their registration cards and name tags and directed them to the refreshment table. It was in a room full of people standing around chatting; everyone appeared to be having a good time. Stevie and Hugo picked up a few snacks; when they turned around, there was Billy with another couple beside him. Billy introduced Stevie and Hugo to Chris and Brenda. "Chris and Brenda are starting a new small group and I just wanted you to meet them," he said.

The two couples talked for what seemed like an hour. They laughed and discussed kids, marriage, home purchasing, and sports. They realized they had a lot in common. Stevie was still suspicious of the church and fearful of what they might think of her, so she did not reveal much about her past.

The few minutes to chat had quickly passed, and the emcee for the evening took the stage to give everyone instructions. It was time to move around the room, pick up some more snacks, and meet more people. Billy came by and took Stevie and Hugo to meet Brian and Jamie.

Brian and Jamie were very friendly. They were seasoned small-group leaders who had just sent out two couples from their group to start a new group. Now they were looking to fill the empty slots at the GroupLife event. Stevie and Hugo felt somewhat out of place with this couple; Brian and Jamie knew a lot about the church and small groups.

The emcee returned to the stage and said it was time to sit down and learn about small groups at LifePoint. Stevie and Hugo immediately looked for Billy and sat with him.

The evening went by quickly and by the end, Stevie and Hugo had met several people. There were people who were new to the church, some who were leading things at the church, and others who were just starting a new small group. They talked with Billy about his group, when and where it met, what would be expected of them, and wondered if they could join his group.

In the end Stevie and Hugo joined Billy's small group. They said Billy was so friendly and helpful that they already felt a bond with him.

A few years have passed, and Stevie and Hugo have become actively involved in LifePoint Church. They serve in various ministries based on their passion and service abilities. Stevie has shared almost all of her life story with the small group, and, to her surprise, they have accepted her without judging her. Hugo enjoys the small group and was baptized by Billy a few months after joining the group.

CONNECTING THE MASSES

The GroupLink event was not LifePoint's first step to assimilation of Stevie and Hugo. A lot of preparation, communication, promotion, and cultural development led to the success of GroupLink.

Telling Stories

Sharing of small-group stories can be seen everywhere around LifePoint — whether it is in a baptism video, on stage, or in the hallway. One of the first questions asked of anyone who calls the church office with an emergency, crisis, or accident is, "What small group are you in?" Small groups are foundational to the life of the church to ensure we accomplish our purpose and objectives.

Building Relationships

Our small-group staff is very relational. In addition to all the story telling, assimilation has a very specific process. The small-group team serves on Sunday to connect people to each other. Introducing people to each other is not only a part of assimilation but a joy for the team. We lead the introductions with three questions: Where do you live? What do you love to do? Who do you know at LifePoint? By having conversations and listening, often these questions are answered without even having to ask. Thus the relationship has begun. If we can discover any kind of association with an existing small group, that is our first connection attempt.

Hobbies and interests have been a very successful way of connecting people for us. As we discover the person's hobbies, we can introduce him or her to others at LifePoint with the same interests. This is not necessarily for an affinity group, it's more about the relationship. The more church members we can introduce to a visitor—especially members with the same hobby—the better chance we have of assimilating that visitor.

These conversations often begin at, but are not limited to, the small-groups booth in the lobby of the church. A visitor or interested person can pick up information about on- and off-campus small groups and complete an information card showing his or her interest in joining a small group.

Strategic Communication

Why do people in your church not know about the happenings at your church? How could someone not know about the GroupLink event at our church? Actually, it's easy. People are bombarded with information on a daily basis, from companies who want their business, from family, from friends, and from the church. Think for a moment about how many times you hear the GEICO or Aflac commercials; very few television programs or radio shows will air to completion without hearing these companies' advertisements. But the church announces something one Sunday and expects everyone to hear it. I seldom hear something that is mentioned once. Oh, I mean I hear it, but I don't *hear* it. It does not stick. Most of the time it does not impact me on the first couple of announcements. Our team discusses often the fact that in America a company will tell *one* message many times. In the church we tell *many* messages one time.

LifePoint small groups have built a lot of media presence about small groups via the website, printed media, and video. Some of this is less in the announcement avenue and more natural around stories of life change. We have by no means perfected the communication process, but having *one message* (every adult is expected to be in a small group for discipleship, community, and service) has helped narrow the focus of what we have to communicate. Discovering how and when to communicate is important.

Assimilating the masses requires clear communication in several avenues. One of the avenues is the church website. More and more people are using the Web to learn about a church before they ever visit. On the groups page of LifePoint's site, we communicate some basics of small group that help people take the next step on the journey of being a Christ follower. Probably the most visited page of information is the one headlined, "Why be in a small group?" (They are also listed at the small-groups booth every Sunday.) These six reasons follow:

1. Understand the Bible better through group discussion as you apply the Bible to your own personal situations.
2. Develop close relationships with other believers who will walk beside you in your journey as a Christ follower.
3. Find answers to the needs in your life through group prayer.
4. Get support in times of crisis or major changes from people who really care for you.
5. Demonstrate to your lost friends the love of Christ in a nonchurch setting.
6. Move from being a spectator to a participant by using your gifts and talents as you serve others.[3]

ADAPT, DON'T ADOPT: THE GROUPLINK PROCESS

You have been reading about GroupLink a lot in the preceding chapters. Early in my small-group ministry I attended one of North Point's married couples GroupLink events. I was honored to have Bill Willits, their small-groups pastor, walk me through the entire process as it was happening, and show me the *why* of every part of the event. I took several pages of notes trying to apply each aspect of this event to LifePoint.

The event you read about in the opening paragraphs of this chapter was from LifePoint's original duplication of North Point's GroupLink. Since then we have continued to adapt the GroupLink event to better fit the life and culture of LifePoint.

LifePoint staff have attended many conferences, read many books, interviewed many ministers, and learned a lot of programs and processes from each other. In the end, we adapt all of the ideas to our history, our culture, and our setting. We adapted GroupLink to a more convenient time for the most people. We now explain GroupLink as:

> a periodic event designed to help you take what can be a scary step into a group and make it more natural and relaxed. A small group is the opportunity we all need to connect with others and continue to grow in God's Truth. At GroupLink, new and existing small groups are available for conversation in the Concourse. You have the opportunity to choose from dozens of groups. Typically, you will select two or three groups with whom to speak. After meeting those groups, you can decide which one you would like to be a part of for Bible study, community, and relationships.
>
> We ask that you commit to this group for a six-week study that will be in conjunction with a sermon series and entire church Bible study. After the initial six weeks, if the group is a good fit, stay connected and grow in your faith together in community. If it is not the best fit, it is okay to step out and try the next GroupLink or let our GroupLife staff help connect you.[3]

GroupLink takes place in the main hallway (the concourse) of the church on a Sunday morning twice a year. Hosts (male or female, single or married) are enlisted and are required to attend host orientation on one of the three weeks prior to the event. (*Host* is the title given to the person who leads the small group for the initial six-week campaign. If a host continues to lead after the campaign, we move that person to the small-group leader category. Host discovery and orientation are discussed in chapter 5.) Each host is asked to first enlist some friends — four couples or eight singles — to be part of the group. Then he or she is able to host a table in the concourse with the assurance of a core. The host is available to talk with potential members in the concourse during all services on GroupLink Sundays. Enlisting friends prior to GroupLink gives the small group a beginning DNA. If a potential host cannot think of at least three couples or four singles he or she could invite, we become concerned about the potential success of the group. Hosting a table at GroupLink opens the group for others to join, but starting with a committed core is a must to increase the chances of success. Announcements, videos, information sheets, postcards, e-mails, and a Web presence about GroupLink all serve together to communicate about the upcoming event. Every visitor and new member who has connected to LifePoint over the last ten months but is not yet in a small group receives a postcard from our pastor describing GroupLink and inviting him or her to participate.

On GroupLink Sundays, which we offer two weeks back-to-back, all attendees to worship services receive a list of new or open small groups whose hosts will be available for consultation in the concourse.

GroupLink is usually offered in February and August around a churchwide study and sermon series. Having the entire church on the same study encourages more people to take the first step toward small group. (The six-week commitment assures they have a way out if for some reason the group is not a good fit for them.) And the discipleship and community that we have seen God produce during these seasons of laserlike focus have been astounding.

The campaign allows small-group leaders to invite friends and neighbors who might not be attending worship on a regular basis (or not attending at all). We were able to celebrate what God was doing through our assimilation process when (on March 8, 2009) our attendance in small groups surpassed worship attendance for the first time in the ninety-nine–year history of LifePoint. This happened during our third churchwide alignment campaign.

Since GroupLink is only offered two times a year, I struggled with how the visitors and newcomers would connect between events. I had been raised and educated on the process of connecting people to a Sunday school class the first Sunday they visited. We'd automatically assign visitors to a class the first time they completed a guest contact card, regardless of their situation or place on their journey. You can't do that with small groups, though, because we treat them like families. Each group has its own issues and meets in homes at various times and days of the week. Situations are different for all small groups.

GroupLink has been such a success that we have introduced a mini-GroupLink in November and April. The mini-GroupLink happens on a Wednesday night in the concourse of the church. Wednesday night programming is designed for all stages of life. The adult portion is focused on helping a person take the next step on his or her journey of being a Christ follower. We offer three classes at various levels on the journey, targeting the beginning, growing, and Christ-centered levels. These classes help draw people who may not be in a small group. The mini-GroupLink serves as an opportunity for open groups to assimilate people who did not or were not able to connect in the six-week campaign earlier in the year.

We have discovered that the retention rates are much higher with a special connection event, rather than just showing someone to a classroom on his or her first Sunday visit. The scheduled event helps people anticipate and gives them a chance to meet before committing. It is no longer about having every visitor assigned to a Sunday school class on paper—it is about success in connecting people.

To help visitors continue to attend LifePoint between GroupLinks, we have several weeks of helpful steps that continue to raise the level of commitment and awareness. A typical visitor will attend services for a few weeks before completing the guest contact card in the bulletin. When the church office receives the contact card, a staff member is assigned to call or send an e-mail explaining the next steps and answer any questions the visitor may have indicated on the card. Next steps include meeting the pastor or speaker of the day at our Pastor's Connection area; inviting them to an upcoming event that might pertain to their interests; and/or encouraging them to attend Discover LifePoint, a one-time class offered on select Sundays. Discover LifePoint informs and explains the purpose, core values, and expectations of membership at LifePoint Church; any other questions are answered as well. Small groups are one of the expectations discussed in every Discover LifePoint class.

Each of these next steps is part of the assimilation process and a way to deepen the relationship and connection to LifePoint. These steps help keep visitors on the journey of connecting with the church and increase the number of relationships they have here. By the time GroupLink Sunday arrives, visitors have gained an understanding of LifePoint and begun many relationships that increase their chances of joining and remaining in a group.

MULTIPLE CONNECTION POINTS

We do not limit ourselves to GroupLink as a way to help people connect with a group. The culture that has developed at LifePoint is one of relationships and connection; multiple connection points are available through various ministries of the church.

Some churches are simplifying connections for newcomers through their websites, using an interactive map with open small groups listed. Visitors can click on the group they desire and be linked to the leader's e-mail to indicate interest. We have chosen not to use this system because we've discovered that most small-group leaders do not sign up to be assimilation directors, so we have instead tried to increase the assimilation through personal communication and relationships. Three methods that work for us are online registration for GroupLink events, on-campus alternatives for those who prefer it, and, of course, the birthing of new groups out of existing ones.

Online Registration

One way we have been successful in connecting people is by keeping the registration for GroupLink open on the website many months throughout the year. This helps with the anticipation and communication of upcoming GroupLink events. By gaining information from the online registration form, it is likely that we are able to connect people to a small group even before the next GroupLink event occurs.

On-Campus Alternatives

Another connection point we offer is an on-campus opportunity, because some adults still prefer to meet on-campus in a traditional Sunday school–style setting. (However, preschool, children, and students are a priority for LifePoint; they learn and grow much better in an on-campus environment. And as these ministries continue to grow, they require more space, so LifePoint has a small amount of space to house adult groups on-campus on Sunday mornings.) We will continue to offer the on-campus option as long as there is space.

On-campus groups look different from the small group that meets in a home. We caution people that this is, in most cases, a very different experience due to the lower level of community experienced by on-campus groups, mainly due to the absence of refrigerator rights (see chapter 2). Nonetheless, a list of on-campus groups, with a brief description of each, is available at the guest-services booths.

In one of my Small-Group Network meetings I heard a friend, Alan Pace, discuss midsize groups. Alan is a fellow small-group pastor who serves at the People's Church in Franklin, Tennessee. In discussing how to help people connect to others and a small group, Alan shared the idea of a supergroup that meets on-campus for a few weeks in order to help build relationships. Then they move off-campus and continue as a small group. We have now made this supergroup an ongoing midsize group on-campus on Sunday mornings. This group is designed to help people connect in a safe, easy-to-access opportunity. It is taught in a master-teacher format, with each table or subgroup of people in the room being lead by a host. Sometimes this host is pre-enlisted, other times the host is discovered in the process of opening questions. From these subgroups we try to start a new small group or add the couples/individuals to existing small groups.

Existing Small Groups Give Birth

As I've stated many times, relationships are very important when connecting people in small groups. Many of the lessons I have learned over the years have come from personal experiences. I never cry when I visit the hospital and see a newborn baby; and it has been a few years, but I don't think I cried at the births of either of my sons. But a birth happened recently that brought me to tears.

A couple had recently received Christ and I had the joy of baptizing them. Almost immediately they joined our neighborhood small group. Each week we had Bible study or an ice cream or pool party. Each week we ministered with and to each other as a group. We prayed especially for our unchurched friends and watched for God to work through them. Eleven months after this couple's baptism, they called and told me they were stepping out of our group. They needed prayer and coaching for their next step. I was in shock. "Why?" They told me about the many people they had been praying for and investing in; many of these people had heard about the new opportunities for small groups in the upcoming churchwide campaign. Their friends had asked them to lead a group for this campaign.

That birth brought tears to my eyes. I do not want to lose my good friends. We have spent months building a deep relationship, serving together, laughing and raising our kids together. However, they were practicing what we had been teaching and encouraging. They were following the natural process of growth. They birthed a new small group with their friends and coworkers and even baptized one of their best friends.

An Eye on Every Visiting Sparrow

Few would disagree that assimilation is a constant part of a growing church, but some seasons and series lend themselves to high-octane growth. For the smaller church, adapting various approaches to assimilation can be beneficial. Our group leaders take seriously the task of identifying new faces every Sunday — to speak to them and offer an invitation to join their group. While this process loses efficiency as a church grows, this eagle-eye intentionality has proven very effective for us.

— Eddie Christenberry, Ridgeview Community Church, Franklin, Tennessee

NEIGHBORHOOD

Don't overlook Matthew 22:39 as you consider how to assimilate more people into small groups: "And a second is like it: You shall love your neighbor as yourself." By loving our neighbors and hosting events, we have seen many people come to small group and become active in church.

Neighborhood groups can be very practical in a mobile society. Most people move every five to seven years and more and more move away from family. Knowing your neighbor has become something of the past. So LifePoint has focused on impacting our communities through neighborhood events, neighborhood ministry, and neighborhood small groups. There are two ways to work in your neighborhood (broadly defined as your community): drawing strangers together for a common event or drawing together people of similar interests.

An Event for Everyone

A few years ago we started a neighborhood small group that originated with an Easter egg hunt hosted by neighbors Larry and Jamie and co-sponsored by LifePoint. At this event I met several new families and began to promote our next neighborhood activity, which was a Fourth of July fireworks show. At the fireworks show I once again watched for God at work.

I identified twelve families that seemed interested in something more, so I invited them to a cookout at my house. At the cookout I suggested the idea of us getting together a couple of times a month to do a small-group–style study of parenting and the Bible. Eight of the twelve families said they were interested in meeting, and our first neighborhood small-group began. Over the next few years, four more small groups multiplied out of this original small group. This same process has been duplicated in other subdivisions throughout our area. This has become a small-group assimilation process in itself. Each spring at LifePoint we teach a two-week class on how to begin a neighborhood ministry and small group.

Similar Interests

The concept of *neighborhood* is not limited to your subdivision. A friend quickly corrected me in one of our annual teachings on neighborhood by saying that his neighborhood was actually the city's tennis courts. That is where he was most evenings and where he was able to build a lot of relationships. So with that we began to include sports, boating, woodworking, motorcycles, hiking, scrapbooking, running, bicycling, and so on in our definition of *neighborhood*. Whatever your interests or hobby, God can use it to connect people for the purpose of drawing them to himself.

You may be thinking this is just another way to start affinity groups, but we do not rally groups around affinity. There are several clubs at LifePoint that are affinity clubs, not having any objective or purpose other than getting together with other people who have the same interests; but the goal is to develop a small group of people from these clubs that take on the objectives of small group.

Here is an example of how we took one person's passion and developed a ministry and assimilation channel out of it. There are people at LifePoint who love baseball. They talk, play, coach, watch, read, and even decorate their office around baseball (the latter being me). One of these men, Charlie Mitchell, is a former Major League Baseball pitcher for the Boston Red Sox who loves to coach and help young players. Around him we were able to begin a ministry called Fielder's Choice. Fielder's Choice is a group of baseball enthusiasts who lead player and coaches' clinics. Each person is actively pursuing a growing relationship with Jesus Christ as they allow him to work through them and use their passions and abilities to share his love. Through the clinics — and coaching local teams — we are able to invest in people, not only for baseball, but for Christ. At the conclusion of one of our clinics, a young coach approached us and wanted to discuss becoming a Christ follower.

> I had not attended LifePoint Church prior to the clinic. Actually I was scared to walk into the big building, but the clinic was something I felt I needed to attend in order to be a better baseball coach. At the clinic, Charlie shared his spiritual journey and I knew I had to talk with him about my similar story. I received Christ as my Lord and Savior and was baptized soon afterwards. Since then I have become active at LifePoint and even joined a small group. If your church had not offered this clinic I might never have come through the doors of the church. Thanks for your service to this community![4]

We have staff and church members who coach baseball, soccer, football, and basketball in the local city leagues as individuals; however, we do not offer sports leagues at our church, even though we have a gym on our campus. This is a leading practice of LifePoint: We will not compete with local organizations that are already doing the activities we are considering. Sports are one of those. Our local community has a large and rapidly growing sports organization from the city as well as the YMCA. Each year these sports leagues ask for more coaches and help with the teams. There was a clear need for the coaches' clinics, which we offer on our campus for many sports throughout the year. The ministry through sports has impacted not only our church, but our community and city, which has made LifePoint's coaches' clinic a requirement for participation.

Recently we partnered with the city to offer more practice fields by giving them access to a corner of our property. Through partnering with local organizations that are already reaching people by providing coaches and clinics, we are beginning and building relationships in our neighborhood. This has been one of the most effective outreaches we have had in community—and it has resulted in seeing people eventually coming to Christ as they join small groups with their coaches and fellow parents.

We have developed another sports avenue: Sunday Chapel for travel teams. We are now offering to lead or train people to lead chapel services for the local travel sports teams who have to play in tournaments on Sundays. As God continued to grow the neighborhood sports ministry, we were blessed to be able to enlist a sports chaplain for this purpose. This has also increased LifePoint's impact on local schools and other sporting organizations.

Obviously the sports ministry of LifePoint is not about getting people in an affinity group. The focus is to ultimately reach people for Christ, but many times this starts with a coach who invites parents to a small group and/or worship service.

What does this have to do with assimilation? Sports and other affinity groups represent a foundational culture of connection that many churches may not recognize as an opportunity for assimilation.

Helping people see that God has wired them with interests and hobbies they can use has become a foundational process at LifePoint.

A fellow minister who was considering starting small groups at his church came to visit and ask questions about small groups. In the two hours we met, much of our discussion was about comparing Sunday school to small groups. Much of the conversation was about trying to understand the benefits, weaknesses, troubles, and other issues involved with adding small groups to their existing options. A recent building program had put them in debt and recent church growth had already filled up the new space. For future growth, something besides building more space had to be considered.

After two hours of conversation, I asked him what he loved to do. He quickly responded, "Elite gun repair." I first thought he meant skeet shooting at the local range, but as he described the high level of specialized repair he did on very expensive guns, I realized he was a specialist and had something to offer his neighborhood. I challenged him to get connected with other hunters and competitive shooters in his church and to consider an outing together during which his expertise could be shared. In events of this nature, the participants often tell others about their experience and the specialist they know. Excitement builds, and soon they are eager to invite their friends to the next event. He commented, "I never thought about using this to reach others."

WHEN CAN I INVITE SOMEONE TO MY GROUP?

Another aspect of assimilation is through friendships with those not connected to your church. About three years into our small-group ministry, people began to get excited about inviting friends to their small group. While this is natural assimilation, we had not trained our leaders on how and when to invite new couples into their groups. Small groups are like families in many respects. The family usually has an understanding about certain things and a key principle or courtesy had not been clearly identified at this point.

This is a courtesy that my mother-in-law taught me. Family members did not bring someone to lunch without giving her warning first. She loved people and loved to help and share, but she did not like surprises. She required the courtesy of you calling her to let her know you were bringing friends to the next family event.

I remember not practicing this same courtesy with my small group. I invited a new couple to our small group without discussing or informing the group. We had prayed for the couple as a group, but I did not discuss inviting them. The new couple showed up at the door and two other couples became very quiet. The small-group experience changed that night and one couple decided not to come back the next week.

I quickly got on the phone and tried to discover what had happened. As it turns out, the couple who did not return the next week had been about to discuss some very personal news with the group, but when the new couple came in, they froze up. They were so hurt because they had finally gotten the courage to share with the group—and then the group changed. They did not know this new couple. The new couple had not yet become family. So the couple who had wanted to open up just stopped attending the group.

A couple of weeks later I was able to work out the situation with the entire group and made a promise to all of them that I would continue to develop relationships with unchurched people, as we all should, but I would not invite them to the small group without talking with the entire group first.

The couple who had stopped attending returned to the group a few weeks later. After a month of group meetings and activities they finally disclosed what they were struggling with and the group was able to walk with them through the problem.

I am sorry it took three years of goofs like this to learn how to help people invite others to their groups, but the lesson will not be forgotten. This courtesy of this assimilation process now is communicated often.

Each month the small group is to have a party—pool party, ice cream outing, white-water rafting, cookout, or whatever. Two out of three of these parties are for the small group to have fun and provide opportunities for families to get to know each other at a deeper level. Once a quarter we ask that this party be for the purpose of inviting the friends you have been building a relationship with who are not in a small group. The entire group is aware of this process. The entire group discusses which party will be designated to bring friends. This enables the group to be part of the assimilation process. These quarterly parties encourage every small-group member to be praying and building relationships. These once-a-quarter parties have been well accepted and become common practice for many groups.

OPEN OR CLOSED GROUPS

The assimilation process is also dependent upon whether you have open or closed groups. As you study various types of small groups, notice that some are very clear about being closed for a predetermined amount of time (twelve, eighteen, or twenty-four months); then the group multiplies and starts new groups. Closed means that no new people can join the group after its initial three weeks. On the other side of the spectrum are open groups. Anyone can attend and join the group at anytime. This would be more like a Sunday school class; the group is open to new people at any meeting.

We have defined LifePoint small groups more with the word *family* than with *open* or *closed*. Some groups are closed for a period of time by their own choosing. We have groups closed to inviting new people to the group due to issues in the group, much like a family. When a couple in the group has mentioned divorce; when a child is going through struggles; when the study is too personal for new people to be involved; when someone in the group has been diagnosed with cancer or other serious illness, groups prefer to be closed. Groups also determine when they are open and can easily assimilate a new person into the group. When groups are open, the coach and coordinator are informed so they can also help guide people to the group.

Assimilation is not a single event. It is not a single-step process. It is not one person's or one division's job. Assimilation must permeate every aspect of your church's life. We help (and I challenge you to help) everyone see that it is their job to help people connect. Whether they work the small-groups booth, help with the GroupLink event, or build relationships in their neighborhood, everyone has an opportunity to assimilate people into small groups.

SMALL-GROUP LEADER

Small-group leaders can have a major impact on the success of assimilating people to new or existing small groups. Each small-group meeting should include time to pray for friends and neighbors who are unchurched. Over time and with continued emphasis, including the quarterly parties for inviting those friends, everyone in the group will feel ownership of the assimilation process. Sharing your small-group story often with neighbors and friends helps them understand the small-group concept. We encourage all small-group leaders to meet new people at the church or in their neighborhood and ask them about their small-group experience when the time is right. Small-group leaders can impact assimilation without enlarging their own group or sending out an apprentice. Through continually telling the story of small group, we celebrate God and people are drawn to him.

A SUNDAY SCHOOL CLASS STORY

An e-mail came in from the teacher of a dynamic senior-adult Sunday school class concerning space. This is really nothing new, because classes often ask for a new room — their room is too crowded or they are concerned about losing their room because of the growth at the church.

This e-mail was different. The teacher asked for ideas on how to get another meeting time for the class. "We are old people with a lot of prayer requests, health stories, grandkid stories, and food," the message began. "It has gotten to the point we don't have time for the lesson and need time to discuss the Bible. Would it be possible to get a room on-campus on Thursday nights for Bible study? We could then use the Sunday morning hour for prayer, food, conversation, and health updates. We would meet in homes, but at our age the women feel pressure to clean the house and cook a full meal. We are practicing as much community as we can at our age."

I laughed at the frankness of his e-mail. However, his desire to help people grow in God's Word without omitting the time for community made me smile too. The class was unanimous in this request and in two weeks began their Thursday night Bible study.

Assimilation can happen anywhere, anytime, at any age. An event at church, a friend at work, a coach of a sports team, or a neighbor who is searching. A class on-campus or a fireworks show in your subdivision or a conversation at the small-groups booth. Adapt, don't adopt, any process about which you read or learn at a conference. Assimilation is a more natural process than we make it out to be. Make assimilation a part of everything you do and allow your ministry to take on the same spirit.

FIVE PRACTICAL STEPS FOR . . .

Your Ministry:

1. List the opportunities you have to communicate the small-group stories of your church.
2. Invite an unchurched friend to church to evaluate what he or

she experiences and what he or she hears about small groups during the visit.

3. Review your website from an unchurched perspective or from the perspective of someone who is attending but not yet connected.

4 What kind of assimilation event could you schedule that will work for your culture?

5. How obvious are small groups in the main foyer of your church? If a visitor wanted to connect to a group, how obvious is his or her next step?

Your Small Group:

1. How often does your group pray for the friends who are not connected to a small group?

2. If you were asked to help assimilate people into small groups, would you know your next step?

3. What are the hobbies or interests of people in your small group? How could you help them start a small group using these interests as a catalyst?

4. Ask your group to decide on a neighborhood to host an event: Easter egg hunt, cookout, campout, fireworks show, chili cook-off, or something else. See what happens next.

5. Do you seek out visitors who come to your church? When you meet them, discover their interests and introduce them to at least three people.

SHARPER THAN YOU THINK (LEADERSHIP DEVELOPMENT)

I had the opportunity to lead one of the workshop sessions for the Saddleback Small Groups Conference a few years ago. It was one of the highlights of my career to fly to California and spend the week with some of the top small-group pastors in the nation. I did not miss a chance to meet new people, sit in on training sessions, and catch the vision that God has for our church. Following the Friday morning plenary session, I was hurriedly making my way across the campus to lead my workshop—"Transitioning Sunday School to Small Groups"—when I received a call from one of our small-group coaches. The call stopped me in my tracks. He sounded frantic and somewhat frustrated.

The coach said one of his small-group leaders had called him about an issue that was going to happen in his small group on Sunday: A new member to the group had called and informed the small-group leader that she was coming to small group on Sunday because she had a demon and wanted them to remove it.

This is not something we usually train for in small-group leader training and development. Up to this point, the leader, coach, and I had only read about such issues, which are an extreme deviation from the normal small-group experience. It was certainly a first for me in twenty-plus years of ministry. How do you train for something like this? While not all matters are as unique as this one, they are all important, especially to the leader.

So how did the leadership development play out in this story? I mentioned I was on-campus with some of the top small-group pastors in the nation. So I immediately started calling them to learn how to respond. In fifteen minutes I was able to return the call to the coach with a plan based on Scripture. We had just run a training event. We had just lived out what we had been teaching and at the same time established a new training model and process.

If a leader has a problem, he is to call his coach for help. If the coach does not have an answer from his experience with many groups, books, or conferences, he calls his coordinator or small-groups pastor.

Not all leaders will attend a training event just because of their faithfulness to the program. Other people will not attend training classes unless they have an issue. (Unfortunately, problems do not always arise when the training is being offered.) Small groups are organic, alive—much like families; they continually cycle through excitement, sadness, stress, and joy. Issues will arise. How you have organized and communicated the training and development will be tested when unusual matters arise.

Being in the education ministry for many years, I have seen a lot of enlistment and training processes and paradigms. Most of my years were in service with the nominating committee, spending weeks during certain seasons enlisting people in order to fill the open positions of ministry in the church. This was a good process that served to accomplish the goals of enlistment at that time.

Those enlisted received mostly on-the-job training, with a training event offered a couple of times each year. For those really dedicated leaders, we sometimes took a trip to a state or national training event. The learning took place not only in the seminars, but also during the break times, chatting with other attendees. These trips were excellent ways to help our leaders experience what it was like in other churches and discuss issues with their peers.

Over the years I have watched and helped lead change in enlistment, training, and development of leaders. Enlistment still has its seasons—although the best enlistment happens through an ongoing sensitivity to God's work in people's lives and discernment when talking with them. We have a few weeks every winter and summer during which we increase the focus on enlistment for the churchwide campaigns, but the success of the enlistment season is improved by the continued sensitivity.

LEADER DISCOVERY

We are constantly watching for leaders to develop out of our own organization. We identify people who are already involved in the ministry and doing the work. Every time we begin to talk about new small-group leaders, coaches, or coordinators, the word *discernment* comes up. Whenever we are standing at the small-groups booth on a weekend, when a person or family approaches and wants to connect to a small group, *discernment* is implemented. Discernment has been foundational for our small-group ministry; we employ it to sense where God is working.

You may be familiar with the author and motivational speaker John Maxwell. Maxwell is one of the leading authors in the area of leadership and works with corporations all over America to develop their operations and leaders. One of our key leadership development tools is his book *Developing the Leaders Around You*. In it, Maxwell devotes an entire chapter to the subject of identifying potential leaders. "Hiring an employee," he says, "is like skydiving: Once you've jumped out of the plane, you're committed."[1] Whether we enlist volunteers as small-group leaders or coaches, or officially hire someone in GroupLife, we must use discernment in making these decisions.

Pilots, Turbos, Apprentices

In chapter 2 I discussed our process of discovering new leaders from pilot groups. Each pilot group should have potential small-group leaders or apprentices they have been training. We meet with these potential leaders and share the vision with them to become small-group leaders. Sometimes we create turbo groups. "Turbo groups are an intensive expression of the Modeling/Turbo phase. These groups are filled almost exclusively with apprentice leaders. It is a turbocharged small group designed to intentionally develop and release leaders, thus starting several new groups at once as it births."[2] There is also the expectation that each small-group leader will have an apprentice to branch out and start a new small group.

Subgrouping

Author and consultant Carl George came by my office in the spring of 2010 to discuss the future of small-group ministry. During our meeting I discovered I had missed some opportunities to implement another approach to starting small groups at LifePoint. Carl asked if LifePoint had any men's or women's Bible study groups that had grown large in number. (These are mostly focused on the material and can grow rather large.) He mentioned that small groups could easily develop out of these larger Bible studies by arranging the room in circles and helping the people in the circles identify a host/leader. This is often called subgrouping. Carl also encouraged me to help the host/leader identify a coleader. This not only increased the number of potential small-group leaders for the future, but guaranteed someone was there to lead the group in the absence of the host/leader.[3]

As it turns out, the night before Carl and I talked we had started a women's Bible study. We had forty-four ladies attend the opening night. The group leader had come by my office just a few hours before Carl arrived. She had been frustrated because she could not get the women to talk and discuss the questions as the material had suggested—so she came by to ask if we could arrange the room in circles, possible even around tables! Of course we could arrange the chairs in circles for her. She left feeling much better about the room arrangement. I did not realize what God had planned until later that day. The next morning I called our women's Bible study leaders and shared what Carl had suggested. LifePoint also has a large men's group that meets every week. We added the subgrouping method to them as well.

In subgrouping, leaders can be discovered through the blink-and-point method. A larger group is formed around a speaker or hot topic for a couple of hours or even a six-week course. This group could be as large as two hundred adults with a master teacher or teaching team. As the study progresses from week to week, the relationships grow deeper among the participants as they sit around tables in groups of six or eight. In the second half of the session or study, the master teacher discusses leadership and group dynamics of sharing the load. He encourages everyone to prayerfully consider whom they would like to follow from among those sitting at their table. On the count of three, participants close their eyes, then open them as they point to the person they want to lead the group. It may sound foolish, but more and more small-group pastors are reporting this practice as another way to help discover leaders.

Jon Weiner, group leadership pastor of Southeast Community Church in Louisville, Kentucky, said, "The advantages of subgroups and discovery of their own leaders are numerous: the group knows each other already, they have chosen their own leader, the leader feels the support of the group, and the group knows it is everyone's responsibility to help the group succeed since they chose the leader together."[4]

As you are reading this, I know what you are thinking: *Yeah, and there are a lot of disadvantages too.* But that's why we offer training. And this is not the only style of leadership discovery that should be used; it is not the foremost plan for identifying leaders. It is, however, a method that has seen higher percentages of leaders attend training—since the group chose them, they feel the responsibility to their friends to learn what it means to lead, and to be the best possible leader. All of these new leaders need clear expectations and training to develop into multiplying leaders. So training and development has to be offered at various times through various channels.

HOST Method

Yet another way to discover new leaders is via the HOST method. My pastor attended a Saddleback Conference and heard Rick Warren say that he offers the opportunity to anyone in the crowd to become a HOST of a small group. Pat returned excited about all the positives of this method and we use it biannually for our churchwide campaigns. By offering *everyone* the opportunity to help their friends, coworkers, and family experience the difference Christ can make in their lives, more people step up to lead. Most of them already know whom they want to invite to their group. At LifePoint, we define the HOST acrostic a little differently from Saddleback.

> *Open your **Home***: Invite four couples or eight singles for six weeks to study the series the entire church is going through. These are people you would like to be with and see them grow in Christ at the same time you are growing.
>
> ***Operate** a DVD player*: We provide all hosts with a free DVD that does the teaching for you. Just play the DVD and watch the speaker with your entire group. Then you can discuss the information from the leader's guide, the book, sermon notes, and DVD information.
>
> ***Serve** snacks*: Food always makes the study go better. After the first week, the leader can invite others to provide the snack for following weeks.
>
> ***Talk***: Most of the participants are the friends, neighbors,

coworkers, fellow teammates, or family that you have invited. Talking should not be a problem.

We encourage hosts to not worry about going deep or chasing issues they don't have answers for—that is why we have coaches, coordinators, and/or staff. The normal procedure is to write down the question, discover the answers, and discuss them at the next meeting.

Here again you are probably thinking this is crazy. You could never imagine enlisting leaders or teachers from the stage by asking just anyone who wanted to step into leadership. I have often heard the response, "We don't know anything about them." Since this is such a true statement, we have implemented a few safety steps along the way to increase the chances of success for the church, the small group, and the new hosts.

We practice our adaptation of the host method twice a year and our pastor is the key enlister in this process. He articulates the importance of being in a group and tells stories about his own small group. We play videos of stories from small groups before or after he preaches. He sends out a postcard to many attendees encouraging them to get connected to a small group or consider helping friends or family around them know more about Christ by being a host. Over a two-week period we have had many people sign up to host who cannot believe they would ever do something like this.

One of our first steps to prepare the new host is to immediately enroll him in the orientation class that is required in order to be a host. Host orientation consists of an interview of the host and basic overview of the expectations for the six-week study. In this orientation we encourage the host to enlist four couples or eight singles with whom he would love to go through the churchwide study. We give him the leader's materials and a DVD of the study. By using a DVD for the teaching, we increase the level of theology and decrease the pressure on the host to be a teacher.

Without prayer and trust in God, none of this would work. Although his plans do not always turn out like ours, these five methods of small leader discovery (pilot, turbo, apprentice, subgrouping, host) have enabled us to continue to grow.

LEADER TRAINING

Many of our first small-group leaders were former Sunday school teachers, which means training had to look a little different because of the style differences in Sunday school and small groups. Our first few small groups told stories about the teacher and the information transfer that they were getting. Little time was offered for fellowship and talking before or after the session. When someone was asked about the group, the response would be more about the topic or title of the book instead of the experience, community, or group dynamics.

Our initial training spent a lot of energy on helping leaders move from seeing themselves as the teacher to seeing themselves as more of a facilitator. We did not want teachers who lectured or spoke more than 30 percent of the time. The training outcome we desired was to see these teachers become facilitators who would lead the discussion of the material or topic and encourage others to speak 70 percent of the time.

For years, our primary training was the weekend training event. Each year the church set aside a Friday night and Saturday morning for church-leadership training. A guest speaker was invited, based on a particular area of expertise, and we would promote the event. People registered to be part of the weekend and attended with excitement. This plan for training was copied by many divisions in the church and worked well many years.

But a couple of years ago this plan failed us. Although we increased promotion and invited a speaker from one of the largest churches and small-group ministries in the nation, the attendance was very low. As many ministers would, I took it personally. However, my team would not allow me to own the lack of attendance. We spent the next couple of weeks evaluating the low attendance by personally interviewing people. The overwhelming response: "People are busy!" Family time is too limited and small group is going well, so folks reasoned, "Why use up a Friday night and Saturday morning in training?" (Particularly since sports are a major attraction in our community and our church, as stated earlier, and these are days when a lot of sports take place.) Two things I learned in the evaluation: (1) Offering training only one time each year increases your chances of people being absent; and (2) We have to offer training and development in a variety of ways at multiple times via various delivery options.

To accomplish the latter, although the idea is somewhat new to LifePoint, we realized that one solution would be to decentralize the church campus and leadership-development efforts. We were able to enlist a former human resources expert to help in the design and implementation of a decentralized development-and-training process. We established our GroupLeader.org website, which is where we house the small-group calendar, expectations, resources, and training information and materials. Thus, while other training options still exist, leaders and prospective leaders are free to access the information at their own convenience (after they've returned home from that Friday night football game). The online training and development process is continually being updated and refined to better meet our needs.

For example, in all our training, we emphasis these six guidelines for small-group leaders:

- *Pray* for God's guidance.
- *Attend* worship on a regular basis.
- *Begin* and end the group meeting on time.
- *Know* the material and direction God is directing you for the group.

- *Study* the Scriptures daily.
- *Apply* the material to your members' lives as you prepare.

We have even added the following Dos and Don'ts of Facilitating:

Facilitator Dos

- Get comfortable with silence.
- Encourage more than a yes or no answer.
- Give affirmation whenever you can.
- Make time to get to know the people in your group.
- Try to involve everyone in the conversations and discussions.
- Know the spiritual next-step needs of each member.

Facilitator Don'ts

- Don't allow gossip or negative talk.
- Don't avoid talking to chronically late people about their tardiness.
- Don't answer your own questions.
- Don't assume everyone in the group is a Christ follower.
- Don't assume everyone owns or knows the Bible.
- Don't teach! Facilitate by talking 30 percent or less.

Host Orientation

Host orientation is designed to share the basic overview of our expectations and answer some of the most common questions concerning hosting a group. We clarify the host expectations with the following list:

- Confess that Jesus Christ is your forgiver, leader, Lord and Savior, and have been baptized.

- Attend HOST orientation before launch day.
- Prepare for each week's study by attending worship and praying through the study.
- Personally invite four couples or eight singles to the group.
- Membership at LifePoint Church is not required to be a HOST. (Membership is required to be a small-group leader; hosts who continue as a leader after the six-week HOST experience are considered leaders and must meet those requirements.)
- It is very important that you show up prepared for each meeting.
- Be sure all materials and equipment are ready.
- Pray for each member by name during the week as you prepare for the session.
- Tell the group that they can help you prepare by praying and attending worship.
- Honor everyone's time by starting and ending on time.
- Let God teach you and direct you as you study his Word.
- Find ways to challenge the group to apply the lesson during the coming week.

These are some of the fears we answer in HOST orientation:[5]

What if no one shows up?

Call everyone a few days before the study to remind them and give them directions. Ask them to bring something to the study like drinks, snacks, and so on.

My house is _____. What will people think?

If your house is relatively clean and everyone has a comfortable place to sit and feels welcome and included, you are good.

I will never remember everyone's name.
No one will remember names, so you should use name tags for the first few weeks.

What if someone asks a biblical question that I cannot answer?

As a HOST or leader, always be honest! It is *normal* not to have all the answers. Let people with difficult questions know you will research their questions and get back with them. Don't wait until the next meeting to respond, though. Call your coach or coordinator and ask for help. Then e-mail or call the person back with your answer. This will probably become the topic for discussion at your next meeting anyway.

What should I do about the kids?

Child care is up to the individual group. Next to assimilation and leader discovery, child care for the group is one of the most talked about issues among small-group pastors. Our best suggestion for child care is to enlist a female student from our church to keep the kids for one hour of Bible study. (Some groups have each family contribute $5 per week for child care.) Rather than giving her cash, however, we suggest you offer to pay her way to summer student camp. You are helping disciple the next generation by guaranteeing her way to church camp.

Bible study is just one hour, although our small-group time is about two hours in length. The kids and babysitter are highly encouraged to eat and hang out around the kitchen with the adults for the other hour. We get to know our babysitter better. She gets to hear and participate with adult conversation about life, God, work, and family. We also get to hear about her life and camp experience, for which we pay. This builds a relationship with the next generation (that goes beyond just keeping your kids out of trouble for the hour) and helps her see what discipleship looks like.

We also sponsor annual babysitting training by the University of

Tennessee Extension Office. We choose a Saturday morning prior to a churchwide small-group launch campaign and offer the five-hour training to all the high school students. Not only do they leave with knowledge of games, proper etiquette, and business understanding, they receive a backpack full of games and equipment with which to lead the child care for a small group. We have also added to this backpack the week's family devotional handouts our church gives each child on Sunday mornings.

How do I feed this group?

- Food is comforting, magnetic, and can be simple.
- Cookies or chips keep people's hands busy, lighten the mood, and give people a chance to chat.
- Coffee after 6:00 p.m.? Don't forget the decaf.
- Share the responsibility by asking someone to help organize the food theme for each week.

Is my house ready?

- **Seating**: Provide a comfortable seat for everyone; every chair should have a back.
- **Temperature**: Remember, too hot = dozing; too cold = squirming.
- **Lighting**: People need to be able to see each other, their Bibles, and study guides.
- **Pets**: Keep them out of sight, out of mind, until after the study.
- **Phones**: Silence ringers and practice a one-hour phone fast.
- **Food and utensils**: Avoid feeling formal. Think paper plates and plastic.

It is in this host orientation that we first discuss the covenant and share the leadership development structure.

A host serves for six weeks in the initial launch of the small group. If he is to continue leading a small group after the six-week launch, he has additional expectations he is required to meet to be a small-group leader. For example:

Small-Group Leader Qualifications

- Be an active member of LifePoint Church.
- Regard the Bible as the God-spoken authoritative guide in your life and faith.
- Hold to the stated vision and core values of LifePoint Church.
- Agree to come into the LifePoint Groups Ministry leadership structure.

Small-Group Leader Expectations

- Build a leadership team; share the load. You are not expected to (nor can you) do it alone.
- Conduct life-changing group meetings. Go in the direction of the study but watch for where God wants to lead you.
- Shepherd the members of your group, love on them like you would want to be loved on.
- Complete the group covenant. This helps everyone in the group have the same direction and cuts down on confusion.
- Develop an apprentice. We all need to share what we know with someone else. At the very least, we need to leave someone behind to take our place.

LEADER DEVELOPMENT

Leader development is an area where I have spent a lot of time working on our strategy and steps. The development process we are practicing, which is organic and ever evolving into the next level, is titled *A123*.

A123

A123 is a progression in development opportunities that help a small-group leader develop as his experience grows as he does the work of God.

A is for apprentice: Some groups will never have an apprentice and may never multiply. But that does not lessen the emphasis on the need for the practice. Every six, twelve, or eighteen months we ask each small-group leader if he or she has an apprentice. This does not require them to send out an apprentice or new leaders often, but it keeps the opportunity in the group's future. It serves as a continual reminder that leaders need to be thinking about the future and growth of the kingdom.

We help develop future leaders by using a process created by Steve Gladen called "Crawl, Walk, then Run."[6] *Crawl* represents giving the apprentice a sentence or question to lead at the next group meeting. As your apprentice becomes more comfortable with this, you move him to the walk portion of apprenticing. *Walk* is the process of letting your apprentice lead a section of the study at the next group meeting. And finally, *run* is letting your apprentice lead the entire meeting. Development happens before and after — but not during — meetings. Enlist the apprentice sometime before a meeting to give basic instruction regarding his or her role in the upcoming meeting. Sometime after the small-group meeting, take your apprentice to lunch and share a positive, encouraging evaluation. This graduated process for your apprentice will help ensure success, and makes it simple for a small-group leader to develop an apprentice.

1 is for one major training event: Each year we have one or two major training or development events. This is where vision is cast, the small-group stories are shared, and celebration happens. The event can be a banquet or even a trip to a training conference; all small-group coaches and leaders know that they are expected to attend one of these events each year. We have even partnered with other churches in our area to help create these training/development events, which conserves travel expenses.

2 is for free lunch twice a year: Each quarter we host a free lunch for all small-group leaders and anyone from their group they want to bring along. For the first year it was something special for only the small-group leaders. We shared stories and cast vision and gave away prizes. Then we entrusted the small-group leaders to carry that excitement back to their groups and inspire them.

During the evaluation time in our GroupLife team retreat, we discussed how we could better help a small-group leader cast vision and help him grow his group. One idea we decided to implement immediately was encouraging the small-group leader to invite the entire small group to the luncheon. What better way could we help the leader cast vision, hear stories of God's work in small groups, discover the next step for the group, and build more unity than to allow all of his group to hear the vision directly from the GroupLife team? Our attendance doubled at the luncheons, and communication improved. We expect every small-group coach and leader to attend (or have his group represented) at a minimum of two luncheons per year.

To continue to thank the leaders individually, we added a once-a-year small-group leader banquet *just for leaders* that celebrates and displays what God is doing.

3 is for meeting with the coach three times a year: A coach works with five small groups on a continual basis. In a ministry that is so grounded and dependent on relationships, meeting together and sharing life and group stories is imperative. It is our expectation that every small-group leader will meet face-to-face with his coach at least three times a year.

While this is the expectation, our experience is that a coach will be in conversation with his small-group leaders much more often than this, whether by phone, text, or e-mail. The coaches are expected to know the stories of all their small groups and conversation is necessary for this to happen. However, the face-to-face meeting is more than just story discovery. It is guided by questions that review the discipleship, community, and service objectives, as well as discuss the future of the group.

One of our key development activities has been to take leaders to lunch. My first summer at LifePoint was spent taking every small-group leader to lunch. There were only twenty-five, some of them former group leaders whose groups had dissolved. These were very informative times of understanding and discovery from a leader's perspective. Lunch is one of the ways a coach can sit face-to-face with a small-group leader and discuss his small-group ministry. Listening is probably the number-one skill needed at these luncheons. But if they think it's an evaluation meeting, most leaders will feel the pressure to quickly make excuses for their group. To help guide the discussion in a positive way we have designed some leading questions. Examples are:

- What is the God story in your group?
- What one thing would you like to see God do in the next three months?
- What is your biggest personal prayer burden? (For example, yourself, your family, your group.)

Don't let yourself fall into the trap of making it harder than it really is. Providing time for conversation (training and development) and resources (books, webinars, websites, DVDs, blogs, and so forth) does not have to be complicated, just intentional. What does your schedule look like this week? Can you invite a small-group leader to lunch?

Leader Development 1

This is the first development material a small-group leader will need to work through with his coach. It was designed to help a host move beyond the hosting of a group to leading the group. This material is organic, constantly being revised as we discover new issues or new ways to communicate it. Leader Development 1 focuses on the learning and discovering that will take place in the life of a small group. It also helps guide the small-group leader to see the larger vision of GroupLife and ministry.

As you design a leadership development plan for your small-group ministry, consider the experience of your team and leaders. Take into account their background and baggage when enlisting them. This will help you target and communicate the proper level of training. Keep the expectations and objectives clear in all development and evaluation processes.

One way we have helped keep the focus of our objectives and expectations apparent is by clearly defining *what success is* for a small group. In all our material we list the church's five expectations as well as the small-group objectives. The success of a small group is based on how well the members feel they are growing in five areas. These five expectations of the church (see chapter 2) or five characteristics of a disciple are the guides for a small-group leader and even influence the curriculum choices for groups.

If you are considering starting a small-group ministry or are new to small-group ministry, the following—our first attempt at a health evaluation—might serve as a guide for starting an evaluation process for your groups.

Discipleship

- Ask group members to talk about the person in their life who has had the greatest spiritual impact on them. Why was that person such an important influence? What was it about that person's character, words, or actions that sparked spiritual growth?

- Instruct group members to think about their quiet times and their level of desire to spend time with God. Have them recall when they felt closest to God and what events or practices were happening in their life at that time.

Community

- Group members should feel a deep connection with others in their group. This connection does not have to be with everyone in the group, but a few close friends. They must make attending the group activities and meetings a priority on their schedule.
- Fun outings can make a tremendous difference in the connection and growth of the group. Consider a white-water rafting trip or bike ride to the ice cream shop this summer. Your group may prefer a pool party or cookout. Through these activities and conversations, God will show you a lot of insight to people, build community, and help you know how to lead.

Service

- As a group, list people who serve in your church. You might want to group them by ministry. Then spend some time praying for these faithful servants. Afterward, ask each group member to choose one or two different people from the list and write them a note of encouragement on behalf of your group.
- Discuss with each member of your group where they are serving, either at the church or in the community. Help each person discover their gifts and passion for an area of service.

- Find a family in the community who needs work done around their house. Gather for a Saturday work party and help with yard work, housecleaning, or painting. Have someone in the group (or from another group) bring lunch over for you and the host family to enjoy together. Explain that this project is an act of love from your small group and church.

These types of questions eventually developed into a small-group health survey. I used Steve Gladen's *Spiritual Health Assessment* to adapt questions suitable for our circumstances. (*Spiritual Health Assessment* can be purchased online at www.smallgroups.net/Small -Group-Ministries-Spiritual-Health-Assessment-and-Planner-(sha) .php.) By taking this survey, a small-group leader can know how the group is doing in regard to the five expectations of the church. Some leaders have taken the survey on behalf of the group; others have actually given a copy to each member and taken the survey in a small-group meeting. Either way, it quickly becomes obvious where the group excels and where it should improve.

As you consider leadership development, think in levels and design a process that will be easily understood. You will want to design a plan to help people move into various levels of your leadership structure so that the ministry can continue to grow.

TRAINING NEEDS DISCOVERY

When we started small-group ministry our focus was on discovering leaders and assimilating people, hundreds of people, into groups. As we became more successful in assimilation, managing the health of the groups became a priority. As the health of the small groups improved, people began to increase their efforts to invite their unchurched friends and neighbors to small groups.

Training: One Size Doesn't Fit All

We are constantly working on different methods to train our small-group leaders, understanding that the one-size-fits-all strategy for training doesn't always work for every leader. We have revaluated our reliance on our Develop One Class – Small-Group Training as the primary means of training for all new leaders. Instead, we have added face-to-face, one-on-one coaching throughout the year, along with online video training to develop both new hosts and existing leaders. The continued growth, development, and replication of our existing small-group leaders are necessary to keep pace with our tremendous growth.

Another goal we have is to make our ongoing training even more effective and practical. We are developing additional "as needed" online video training for existing leaders as well as for the basic training that all new leaders need when they start leading a group. We believe a healthy combination of face-to-face training and coaching, combined with leveraging the best of the new social networking tools for communication will help us reach our goal of staying connected with thousands of small-group leaders as well as enable us to help individual leaders continue to grow and develop in the future.

— David Hull, Woodlands Church, The Woodlands, Texas

The practice was based on Luke 5. Levi was called to follow Jesus; as he did so, his life was forever changed and he wanted all his friends to know Jesus as well. So he threw a party and invited Jesus and invited all his friends:

After this he went out and saw a tax collector named Levi, sitting at the tax booth. And he said to him, "Follow me." And leaving everything, he rose and followed him.

And Levi made him a great feast in his house, and there was a large company of tax collectors and others reclining at table with them. And the Pharisees and their scribes grumbled at his disciples, saying, "Why do you eat and drink with tax collectors and sinners?" (Luke 5:27-30)

Today this type of response is known as a Matthew party, and these have become a foundational element in small-group growth. And these parties have increased the number of yet-to-be Christ followers in groups.

We then discovered a lack of confidence in small-group leaders in helping someone cross the line of faith. We responded to this lack of confidence with many individual lunches, blog posts, online information, and a couple of resources which groups could use to help everyone with this issue.

By *spending time* with your leaders you will discover development and training needs. You can choose whatever resources you and your church are comfortable with, but the point is to address the issues very clearly. By doing so, you will not only help a leader but also establish the assurance that issues will not be ignored. It's important to establish this trust in the ministry itself, so that leaders know they have backup.

In *Developing the Leaders Around You*, John Maxwell discusses UCLA's successful basketball coach, John Wooden. Maxwell says that Wooden was a winner because he "knew that if you oversee people and you wish to develop leaders, you are responsible to: 1) appreciate them for who they are; 2) believe that they will do their very best; 3) praise their accomplishments; and 4) accept your personal responsibility to them as their leader."

Maxwell also quotes Bear Bryant: "If anything goes bad, I did it. If anything goes semi-good, then we did it. If anything goes real good, they did it."[7] Developing leaders means sharing the load, giving credit often, saying thank you continually, and helping those leaders for whom you are responsible to lead see their own potential.

Take Maxwell's quotes to heart and see how these might change your ministry. Spend time with your leadership team and small-group leaders to thank them and appreciate them.

SMALL-GROUP LEADER

Leadership development begins with apprenticing. If you are a small-group leader, the first question to ask yourself is, "Do I have an apprentice?" If so, what are you doing to help him be all God intends him to be in leadership? If not, I suggest you spend time right now in prayer for an apprentice in your group. Prayer is one of the key steps in discovering an apprentice. Among your group, whom should you be praying for and investing in to help step up in the leadership role? Whom do you sense God leading you to ask to come alongside you to learn and lead?

Once you have begun to apprentice someone toward leading a group, consider what areas of your own leadership role you need to develop. Each of us can sit back and get through the next small-group meeting with a good DVD and a study guide, or with at least a couple of people who like to talk a lot. But that isn't the way to do it.

You have probably experienced the ill-prepared leader who can ask a couple of good questions and the meeting time spins away, without really going anywhere. That is not leading people to experience the objectives of small group. If there are topics or issues you avoid or feel inadequate discussing, talk with your coach or small-groups pastor about how to help your small group move forward—and how you can develop your leadership potential.

I hope you have sensed, reading this chapter, that as the small-group leader, you are the recipient of a lot of time and energy that is focused on training and development. Many of the small-group pastors or point people try diligently to discover what issues you deal with in a real, live small group. All of us should be involved in a group and learning from our own experiences; however, these are not *your* experiences. Only *you* can share with your coaches and pastors what issues concern you. Take the initiative to be involved in the training, development, and coaching opportunities your church provides. These will give you much-needed foundational practices that will help you realize all God has for you, as well as respond to the issues that may arise in your group. You may still see a problem or two that leads you to call your small-group pastor (even if he is away at a conference). For those times, let God work through the phone call and the experiences of your coach and pastor.

DEVELOP MULTIPLYING LEADERS

One of the unwritten practices at LifePoint is to never travel alone—always take with you someone in whom you are investing. As a small-group pastor or point person, what are you doing to help your leaders and potential leaders to take the next step? You can't take everyone to a conference, but when you go, don't miss the opportunity to develop others by taking someone with you. The level of development and training that the people receive when they travel with you is rarely available in a book or local training event. They return with a vision to multiply not only themselves but also others in their ministry. You shouldn't miss any chance to grow leaders by taking them to conferences with you. Without the continued development of more leaders, our organic ministry of discipleship, community, and service will not survive. (And for some, the future of your career may depend on it.) As the leaders develop, we encourage them to develop others.

Multiplying leaders are those who see the kingdom of God as something bigger than their local small group. These leaders understand the opportunity they have to impact the lives of their friends, family, and neighbors. Multiplying leaders know that in the next six, twelve, or eighteen months their coach will be asking about an apprentice and the need for another small group. They realize that this is not about them, but through their obedience to let God work through them they will see him grow more leaders to share the love of Christ with others. According to the Great Commission: "Go therefore and make disciples of all nations, baptizing them in the name of the Father and of the Son and of the Holy Spirit, teaching them to observe all that I have commanded you. And behold, I am with you always, to the end of the age" (Matthew 28:19-20).

Jesus: The First Multiplying Leader

As I was researching the multiplication of leaders and groups, I discovered that LifePoint's GroupLife assistant, Charity Smith, has an enthusiasm for developing multiplying leaders. These are her thoughts on the best example of a small-group multiplying ministry.

Quality leaders are a crucial part of every ministry, especially in a division like the small-group ministry, in which you need a leader for every twelve people. Even though developing leaders is not always an easy task, it is a required one. Jesus commands in the Great Commission to "go and make disciples" and as long as Christians are obedient by adding to the kingdom, there will always be a need for leaders to disciple and mentor them. Paul further enforced this command by encouraging leaders to find potential trustworthy leaders to mentor when he said, "and what you have heard from me in the presence of many witnesses entrust to faithful men who will be able to teach others also" (2 Timothy 2:2).

The most significant example of a leader who spent time walking alongside new leaders and encouraging them to go and do the same is Jesus, who did this with the twelve apostles. Jesus spent a majority of his time during his earthly ministry developing these twelve individuals. He knew he had a limited time to shape their attitude, values, actions, and character. He wanted them to portray him to the rest of the world; the disciples could not learn to be him by reading about him. They needed to be shaped by him, spending time with him in a personal relationship.

Valuable character building results from moments when you

are hanging out, eating together, sharing your hobbies, and getting to know the family. Have you ever noticed the more time you spend with someone the more you imitate his or her characteristics? After you're around someone for a length of time, you begin to pick up — whether good or bad — their outlook, morals, and even some of their mannerisms. Christ did not want a poor representation of who he is. He wanted individuals who would be *his* hands, feet, and mouth.

Fortunately, Scripture gives us a game plan for how we are to do this. Jesus invited some people and others, like Andrew, went to him. Jesus didn't select people who were established leaders in the community. Instead, he selected those he knew had potential to be great leaders. Also, he "spent the night praying to God" (Luke 6:12, NIV) before he invited them to be one of his apostles. The important piece of information here is Jesus took his time observing and praying before he recruited these men. Take your time before inviting someone to lead, because sometimes it is the person you would least expect in your small group who has the capability of becoming a great leader.

After Jesus put his dream team together, he spent time developing them. He instructed them and he looked for those teachable moments. Peter always seemed to be the receiver of most of those. Maybe he was a visual learner. Jesus also gave them opportunities to step up to the plate and do some of the actual ministry. Allow your apprentices to take the lead occasionally and facilitate the lesson or organize the next service project (see Crawl, Walk, Run). Not everything can be taught by instruction. Some things are learned better when you do the work yourself.

Then Jesus sent them out (Matthew 10:5). He never expected these men to remain where they were. He didn't spend all that time developing these leaders so they could remain together. They became great friends and brothers, so it had to be extremely painful for them to leave each other. Nevertheless, the growth of the kingdom depended on them leaving what was comfortable and allowing the Holy Spirit to stretch them even further. Sending someone who has cried and laughed with you out of your group can be a difficult experience, but standing in the way of another's opportunity to disciple and do all that God has called them to do is even more difficult.

It takes much more than your willingness to develop multiplying leaders. You need to never stop trying to grow spiritually so you can continue to pour yourself into them. You need determination to walk with them for a lifetime, if needed. And you need to live a genuine, pure lifestyle that your protégés will be challenged to match. Don't underestimate the importance of the call to mentor. People's lives will be impacted well beyond your area of ministry. Even though this is not an easy task to take on, the rewards are well worth it. You get the satisfaction and joy of watching someone grow into the man or woman of God that our heavenly Father intended them to be. You may never know while you live on this planet who will be impacted because you were willing to invest some of your time and energy into another leader, but one day you will, and it will be well worth it.[8]

As I've noted, developing small-group leaders is a never-ending cycle of discovery, training, and development. Nonetheless, the process of learning as issues arise is a rewarding one, for ministry leaders and those they are developing. And without this ongoing process, I am convinced many churches will struggle to survive.

FIVE PRACTICAL STEPS FOR . . .

Your Ministry:

1. Review your enlistment process. Are there opportunities to include basic training for these new leaders?
2. What large groups are already meeting in your church that

could be subgrouped for potential small groups?

3. What are the expectations for small-group leaders in your church? Are they clearly communicated?

4. Review your last three years of training and development opportunities. Do you see a variety of information as well as multiple delivery options?

5. Write a list of training issues that you see in small groups. Design a development process to address these.

BONUS: Take someone to lunch this week.

Your Small Group:

1. Leadership development begins with apprenticing. Do you have an apprentice?

2. Who are five or six people around you that you could help develop?

3. If you could have lunch with anyone in your small-group ministry to discuss small-group life, who would it be? Why not call that person and invite him or her to lunch?

4. Do you have a way to gauge the health of your small group? If so, do this in your next small-group meeting.

5. Are you involved in a midsize group Bible study or ministry? What can you do to help guide people in this group or ministry toward joining a small group?

HIGHER THINKING, NOW (CURRICULUM CHOICES)

He was a minister of education who had been very successful in growing Sunday school in various churches throughout his career. This same success had filled his current building, and people continued to be excited and God continued to add to the number attending his church. The church decided to build another building, most of it being for education space. By the time the building was complete and the several million–dollar bank loan had to start being repaid, the building was full. Children and preschoolers had taken over most of the space designed for education. It seemed that every adult who came to the church had at least three children — but it felt more like ten. And people continued to bring friends, and the building was overcrowded. It was not long before the rapid growth slowed down. Then the attendance began to decline in Sunday school and worship began to plateau. He had to do something, so he called some friends and ended up in my office to discuss the option of off-campus small groups.

Since I had been in his role as minister of education for many years and talked with many other ministers of education about small groups, I knew some of the questions he would be asking. It wasn't long into the conversation that the subject of curriculum and control emerged.

I almost have to laugh now when I think about how we (ministers of education) think we have control of what goes on in the group, whether off-campus or on-campus, just because we supply the curriculum for the groups. I had fought this same battle in my heart, head, and ministry just a few years earlier.

I told him about the first time I had to help a small group with curriculum choices. In the early 2000s, Rick Warren's *The Purpose Driven Life*, a forty-day churchwide campaign, had swept the nation. Thousands of churches had started small groups around this study and let groups meet off-campus for the first time in the history of the church. The study brought life change for people and churches in those forty days. However, day forty-one came and many of us did not know what to do next. Many groups wanted to continue to meet in homes at times that were convenient for them. All of them were asking, "But what do we study next?" Leaders of some of the groups found a good subject online or went to the local bookstore and purchased a book. Other groups let their members search out subjects and books they wanted to discuss. One group I spoke with asked a member to go to the local bookstore and purchase several copies of his choice of study for the group. He purchased *The Survivor: Bill Clinton in the White House* by John F. Harris. Why? Because when he entered the bookstore there was a large display of the top ten books. *The Purpose Driven Life* was first and *The Survivor* was second. Bill Clinton was a hot topic then, and it was next to *The Purpose Driven Life*. I guess it made sense to him.

Then I told him about another situation, in which an on-campus group had abandoned the church-approved study. The teacher had purchased another study on his own and did not ask or tell anyone except the class that they were doing this study. The class did not know it was not part of the church curriculum. During class time the teacher was stating his own opinions and his own theology, which was *not* that of the church. He was contradicting the pastor and teaching against the church's practices. This happened on-campus during a Sunday school hour.

The point is this: We really do not have control of what goes on in a class or group just because we provide, buy, or suggest the curriculum.

There is a lot more to helping a group or class move in the right direction via study guides and materials than just who purchases it.

In the Southeast, yet another way of curriculum discovery exists; we call it the "Brother-in-law in Florida" method. Let me explain. I was a young minister of education in charge of the Sunday and Wednesday night classes we called Discipleship Training. Every fall and spring I would design a course booklet with all the studies that would be available on-campus. We offered six-week, ten-week, and thirteen-week classes. I was so proud of all the opportunities for people at our church to grow not only in the knowledge of God's Word but in the "renewing of their mind" (see Romans 12:1-2).

One night about mid-semester, a friend stopped me in the hall and showed me a book he felt we needed to offer. "My brother-in-law in Florida just finished this study and says our entire church just has to go through it," he said. I smiled and took a look at the book. "Never heard of it," was my response. Then I asked if I might take it and review it.

The next day my pastor came into my office for something and noticed the book on my desk. "Where did you get that?" he asked. When I told him, he responded that the book had been blamed for several heated discussions and a few church splits. That was my lesson on book suggestions from family members (or from anyone for that matter). I will not offer a book just because someone has recommended it. Each book suggestion is reviewed for an approximate two-week period; if it's biblically based and in line with our philosophy and theology, as well as the DNA of our church, we will try to position it into our study options.

SPIRITUAL FORMATION

Spiritual formation is much more than just what curriculum you choose to use. The curriculum has an impact on each person's journey and is a very important element, but it is only one element. Spiritual formation as described in Romans 12:1-2 requires more planning and processing:

> I appeal to you therefore, brothers, by the mercies of God, to present your bodies as a living sacrifice, holy and acceptable to God, which is your spiritual worship. Do not be conformed to this world, but be transformed by the renewal of your mind, that by testing you may discern what is the will of God, what is good and acceptable and perfect.

This subject has led us to put a lot of emphasis on curriculum designs and choices. We strive to help people along the journey to be more like Christ—next week or next year—than they are today. This is dependent upon the Holy Spirit, the individual, and our plan or study options. However, having a goal for each individual in your church as to where you want him to go or what you want him to become will help guide the choices you offer. What is the target for people in your group or church? How can you help them get there as you journey along together? What options for curriculum will you offer?

THE JOURNEY

The Reveal research done at Willow Creek Community Church uncovered how well the church had been making disciples. They spent months surveying the congregation and many more months analyzing the results. When they asked people (in many different ways) how they would describe their spiritual lives, a "spiritual continuum" emerged.[1] This sequence was determined by experts to be one of the most highly predictive models they had seen. It centers not on church activities, but rather on a growing relationship with Jesus Christ. The spiritual continuum is divided into four categories: exploring Christianity, growing in Christ, close to Christ, and Christ-centered.[2] We have personalized (renamed) these categories for our church and used this research to guide not only our curriculum and resources for small groups but also our church disciple process. We call it the Journey.

By using the word *journey* we emphasize the fact that we are constantly in motion to become more like Christ. As you read each description, consider the people leading your small groups as well as those attending them. Consider the people who attend worship each week or those who serve in various ministries of your church. Try to surmise which percentage of your congregation falls into each category and let this information guide you in your planning.

- The *Exploring Christianity* stage declares, "I believe in God, but I'm not sure about Christ. My faith is not a significant part of my life."
- The *Beginning* stage says, "I believe in Jesus and I'm working on what it means to get to know him."
- The *Growing* stage is one of the hardest steps to take and it is defined with, "I feel really close to Christ and depend on him daily for guidance."
- The *Christ-Centered* category says, "God is all I need in my life. He is enough. Everything I do is a reflection of Christ."[3]

Each of these categories can have an impact on what studies you offer. As you determine the percentages of each category that are represented in your church, consider how small groups and discipleship classes can work together to help move people to the next step on the continuum.

Have I mentioned that I love baseball? I am an assistant coach for a travel baseball team. Our head coach, Chris, is very knowledgeable on the sport. When our team is successful in executing a new play at an important time in the game, he will look at me and smile, and I know his thought is, *Now that was higher thinking*. "Higher thinking" is a phrase he has coined for his process of thinking ahead of the game. There are very few moments in a game in which I can have conversation with him about a previous play. (I do like to analyze and talk.) They are very few because he is thinking two or three batters—or even two or three innings—ahead. While I, the other personality, want to discuss and celebrate the past three outs.

Chris has taught me a lot about coaching baseball. But this lesson is not just for the baseball field. Higher thinking can and should be applied to life and ministry.

Higher thinking is what many schools and religious organizations put into their scope-and-sequence planning. Designing a plan or curriculum choice allows people to see what foundational elements are important to their spiritual formation. Scope and sequence in the academic setting puts emphasis on the material or information. When we add in the needs, personalities, and the location on the spiritual journey of those who will be studying and being discipled, we have brought life into the curriculum choices. Applying the higher-thinking practice will help you and your ministry team guide the journey, somewhat, via study choices.

For many years, I left out a key element of curriculum choosing—the DNA of our church. In this case, DNA can be defined as the location of people on the spiritual journey to be more like Christ, combined with the social, economic, and cultural makeup of the people of your church. When you think about the average person in your church, what is he or she like? What is his average age? How long has she been a Christ follower or attending a church? What is his education level? These types of questions can guide you toward DNA discovery. Then add the expectations and the core values of your church to this DNA.

If your church has not defined the core values and expectations, that is okay. You can still design study choices around a basic framework. Gather your team for a discussion about what they think are the core values and expectations for your division or ministry. Then begin to choose resources for each of these expectations.

You are now on your way to developing a curriculum guide.

CURRICULUM GUIDE

A curriculum guide gives small groups options and power to choose their next study, but keeps the parameters in line with the church's theology and philosophy. It is a loosened control from purchasing the material for every class or group, but it is still a guide.

When evolving our curriculum guide, which is organic (that is, results from our own observations) and is edited approximately every six months, we developed an equation to influence our choices. This equation is: (1) the church's DNA + (2) the five expectations + (3) our core values = core curriculum. Each of the five expectations (remember, for LifePoint they are worship, biblical community, service, influence, and generosity) has three core study choices from which to choose. The three studies are written at different levels and various study styles. We also added electives for a mixture of studies that lined up with the church's ministries — marriage, parenting, women, men, and Bible book studies.

The curriculum guide is posted online, given out at each small-group luncheon, and available in our bookstore in the small-group studies section. Leaders can review the choices, share the list with their group, and discuss what to study next. This process gives the small-group leader more responsibility and gives the group more ownership of their spiritual growth.

Every week, someone stops me or one of our GroupLife staff in the hall at church and asks, "What study should we do next? We just finished . . ." and she names some study. If you have been leading a group for a few weeks or a few years, this is still a common question. We direct this person to the bookstore located in the church, which has many of the current suggestions on display. However, there is a little more to selecting your next study than shirt or shoe shopping at your local retail store, and we understand that. We have put hours into designing and researching the choices. And most of the bookstore employees have had a brief overview of how to help someone decide on which study to do next.

When we began offering the curriculum guide, several small-group leaders would still stop one of our staff, hand over the curriculum guide and ask, "What study do you think we need to do next?" Now this is funny to even think about, but when it first happened, my first thought was to throw the guide down and walk off. We had spent hours reviewing the choices to offer. We had printed a few rough drafts that we circulated among the staff for editing and suggestions. We then printed a hundred guides and gave them out everywhere we saw small-group leaders. And still they would hand it back to us with this same ole question.

HEALTH SURVEY

We realized we had to do something else. Just offering a list of titles was not enough. Some publishers of small-group resources will categorize the studies for various levels of spiritual maturity. This is helpful when building your curriculum guide.

Then I read the *Spiritual Health Assessment and Spiritual Health Planner.*[4] It is designed to help a small-group leader know his group's spiritual makeup. This assessment method also gave suggestions for studies and activities to help a person grow in the five purposes. From this material and discussions with Rick Howerton and Steve Gladen, we were able to develop our own health survey. This is a quick review of the five expectations of LifePoint Church. In a matter of minutes, a small-group leader—or even the entire small group—can conclude where the group is strong, where it needs improvements, and see suggested studies to grow their group in the weak areas. "What do we study next?" is no longer a question for our leaders; the group can discuss it and then be guided toward resources.

You don't have to have a bookstore in order to offer resource options for your groups. Our bookstore started as a shelf in the hallway outside my office. It then moved to a corner of the library and the librarian was trained in how to help people decide on a resource for their group. The resource area grew to the point that more and more people purchased their small-group studies; library books were no longer being checked out. Most people said they would rather buy the book and be able to write in it and keep it for the future as a reminder of God's work in their lives. It becomes a journal approach for them.

As I wrote this chapter, four years after starting the curriculum guide, I received an e-mail from our bookstore manager asking for more curriculum guides. The small-group leaders had taken most of them from the bookstore to discuss the study options with their groups. I guess I should have asked for forgiveness for my frustration in the early years.

CALENDAR FOR SEASONS

There are seasons for certain studies that seem to be more natural than others. We have designed a suggested calendar of study topics and activities or parties for groups to help them think ahead.

Every spring we begin to prepare the groups for summer activities. We have chosen to not offer on-campus adult studies on Wednesday nights during June and July in order to give adults the opportunity to reach out in their street, subdivision, or community. In preparation for the summer we suggest neighborhood ministry ideas as well as studies in sharing Christ.

The churchwide campaigns are another season of study. LifePoint has made a commitment to have two annual GroupLinks combined with a churchwide sermon-and-study series in which we expect every small group, whether on- or off-campus, to participate. The suggested calendar lets the groups know when these two studies are happening so they can schedule around this period.

You can also include activities for the community-building objective of small groups as well as service projects throughout the year. This calendar is available online and at each small-group luncheon. Helping groups plan ahead is part of leadership and guides them when choosing studies.

WRITE YOUR OWN

Early in my ministry I felt like there was a better way to have a Bible study than buy a book. *Surely I could write a study as good or better than those big companies*, I thought. How hard could it be? You just use what the pastor is preaching, write a few questions, and discuss at your group that week. I even went as far as enlisting other like-minded people to help me come up with questions during the sermon. We would compile our thoughts after service and be on our way to lead the "best small group ever." Well, that lasted about six weeks: I was absent from worship for a mission trip . . . My like-minded friends were either on vacation or forgot to e-mail the questions to our apprentice for that afternoon's study. The groups gathered and had no material from which to discuss, two of the five couples had not even gone to worship that week, and the other two didn't attend church at all. Then I had a revelation. I am not *hired* nor *wired* to write small-group material!

So we tried a different track. These like-minded friends and I decided to meet with the pastor to learn of his direction for sermons for the next few months. Then we searched (online) the two or three companies that we trusted for resources and found three studies that lined up with the direction of the sermons. We went to our bookstore and had them order these study books for our groups. Now, whether we are there or not, able to attend worship or not, have group members who attend church or not, groups are able to still have Bible study. I am able to focus on ministry, assimilation, and care. And, by the way, that is what I was hired to do!

Questions on Curriculum

I encourage group leaders to look for material that is relationally-oriented, manageable in size, and takes a creative multifaceted approach to communicating its content. I also advise they look for material that has good open-ended questions designed to stimulate discussion and actually expresses it has the goal of building relationships among participants in addition to learning the content of the curriculum. Last but not least, it's important group leaders try to find material that aligns with their church's core values, vision, and strategy for fulfilling their shared mission.

Remember: Curriculum is meant to serve the group — not the other way around. First, group leaders should get a picture of what the Lord wants them to do in the group (vision). Then choose curriculum that will serve that end. Always be flexible and always be prepared to scrap the curriculum if it feels like the energy of the group is waning.

— Reid Smith, core director of adult ministries at Christ Fellowship, Palm Beach, Florida

RESOURCES

Another issue that has evolved is the purchasing of resources for the small group. For many years, probably generations, the church bought Sunday school quarterly books for teachers and members. We budgeted for each person in each class to receive a new study each quarter of the year. That was a good way to guarantee the members would have material to prepare for class. At the end of each quarter I would collect the outdated literature and restock for the next quarter. Many times I would find a lot of the books we had ordered for the class still in the room after the material had run out of date; it was upsetting to see such a waste of funds and resources on books that were never used.

Then we began small groups in which each group has the power to choose their own study and length of time they want to study it. Along with the church growth we were experiencing and the economic changes that impacted our community, our budget could not keep pace with the growing need for resources. We began to change the way we offered literature.

The choices and styles of resources are many. Depending on the type of study, we try to partner with small groups on the cost of resources. For the DVD-led studies, we purchase the DVD kit and leaders can check it out from our bookstore. For churchwide campaigns, we provide the leader guides and DVDs for all leaders. Participants then each buy the book (as noted earlier, most people tell us they prefer to buy the book so they can write in it). If there is a hardship case or an expensive study that must be offered, many times the church is able to share the individual cost of the resource.

SMALL-GROUP LEADER

You have probably been in the what-study-do-we-do-next situation. If you stop one of the LifePoint staff with this question on a busy Sunday morning, we quickly direct you to the small-group studies section of our bookstore and the curriculum guide. However, seeking guidance is a fine idea.

First, I suggest that you e-mail or call your coach or small-group pastor during the week—when he can talk without interruption and you can discuss the story of your group. It is a joy to hear about what God is doing in the life of a small group! This also allows him time to review some options with you and help you make the choice. This e-mail or phone call is not an evaluation of you or your leadership; it is to help with the decision concerning the next study.

Second, prayerfully consider what areas of your group seem to be going well. The focus will be on the main objectives of a small group for our church, which are discipleship, community, and service. Every group will do very well in one of these areas and most of the conversation will be about how well you are doing in this area. However, every group will need improvement in one of these areas and will avoid talking about it. (If you call me, I usually suggest you target one of your group's need-improvement areas.)

Third, use your in-house health survey (we developed ours from the Steve Gladen *Spiritual Health Assessment* noted earlier) to help discover areas your group may be lacking. There are hundreds of resources to help move people along their journey in specific areas. We have trained our bookstore employees to share this survey with those who ask what study to do next.

Once you have identified the areas — whether by taking the survey yourself or having each member of the group take the survey — you can compare the results to the curriculum guide for suggested studies in that particular area.

Curriculum choices are more than information transfer; Romans 12:1-2 tells us they involve "the renewal of your mind." A master plan of resource choices and a goal for where your church wants people to go is important, but as the small-group leader, you are the shepherd of the group. You know which of the expectations or objectives your group struggles to live out. You don't lecture; you facilitate God's leadership in the group by being aware of the goal. You don't drive or demand; you help guide. You have the prescription your church has mapped out via curriculum choices for the next steps on the journey. The next study or discussion guide is for deepening relationships — relationships with each other, but more importantly, relationship with Christ.

Your role as the small-group leader at this point is as important as the communication from the front lines of a battlefield. Without your insight, without your efforts to tell the story of what God is doing in the group, a choice for the next study would be just about information. Take seriously the what-study-do-we-do-next question. Share with your coach, coordinator, or small-group pastor (via e-mail, a phone call, or over lunch) what God is doing in the group. Review the expectations, core values, and objectives of your church and groups ministry. In light of that information, seek out your next study through prayer and counsel to help your group move along the journey to being more like Christ.

Another aspect for you to remember concerning curriculum preparation comes from a Twitter posting from Rick Howerton in April 2010: "It is not how well you prepare the material for the small-group lesson. It is how well you listen to God in respect to each person in your group as you prepare the material."[5]

Author and consultant Carl George spoke at a Small Group Network luncheon during which he challenged us with six questions. These questions might also help you in your quest as a small-group leader or small-group pastor:

- What is God doing among the people in your group?
- What are the challenges your members are facing?
- How is the group helping them with these challenges?
- What challenges are you facing as you help these people minister?
- What are you trying to do, really?
- How are you getting in the way of what you want to happen?[6]

We all strive to be the best small-group leaders possible. Sometimes a little glance into our group or our own hearts with these types of questions may take us to a new level of "best." The answers to these questions may just determine your next small-group study or leadership direction.

MY STORY

My small group had become like family. The group was comprised of couples who were either new or not yet Christ followers. Most of them had not grown up in church but were intelligent on many matters of the church. They were able to carry on conversations at deep levels about life, leadership, and family. However, very few had spent much time in Bible study. After six months of my teaching or inserting the teaching DVD and then discussing, I felt like I was doing the talking at least 50 percent of the time. I asked the group what they wanted the focus to be for our next study. The response: "We love it when you tell us the history or explain the Bible so we can better understand the setting and situations they are writing about. None of us really know the Bible."

However, there was not a "Bible 101" study on our curriculum guide. I contacted a few fellow ministers and asked for their suggestions. Several books were reviewed before we landed on one that would meet our group's needs. Two weeks later we had our first meeting. To my surprise each couple had purchased the book and begun reading it before our meeting. They were involved in the material before the meeting because they had ownership in the choice and were interested in the content. In terms of discussion and the high level of interest, this meeting was in the top two of the best we'd had since our inception nine months earlier. On another day, I dropped by Wes's house to pick up my son (Wes is in my small group). As I prepared to leave, Wes said, "Hey, I have a question." He pulled out our study book and began to discuss the Old Testament books and asked about primary and secondary books. We discussed. We researched from the Bible. We discovered answers to his questions and learned new information about the Bible. As I was leaving, I smiled and thought about what had just happened. *This* was what small-group family is all about. We had chosen the right study.

You can make great curriculum choices, too, with a little fore-thought and care. Knowing the complex characteristics of your church and the small groups that spring from it should be what guides decisions in this arena.

FIVE PRACTICAL STEPS FOR . . .

Your Ministry:

1. Define spiritual formation in your church.
2. Gather a team to write a small-group health survey or purchase Gladen's *Spiritual Health Assessment and Planner* for your ministry.
3. How are resources or classes categorized for various levels of spiritual maturity in your church?
4. What is the DNA of your church? Has this impacted your curriculum choices?
5. Discover one resource that you feel must be studied by every small group. Tell them.

Your Small Group:

1. Do you have the e-mail address and phone number of your small-group pastor and/or small-group coach?
2. Ask your small-group pastor or coach to help you evaluate a new resource before you start using it with your group.
3. What is God doing among the people in your group? Share the story.
4. Have group members taken the health survey to determine the next study for your group?
5. How well are you listening to God as you prepare for the next small-group meeting?

NOW WHAT? (DEVELOPING ISSUES IN SMALL-GROUP MINISTRY)

You may have been in small-group ministry for many years, a few years, or are just considering this style of ministry. Small groups is not a program but a life we are called to live with others. Over and over you hear stories of life change, real transformation that can only come from God. But being there—doing life in a small group of people—when it happens is exciting.

TIMELESS PRINCIPLES

Your first decisions and questions are crucial to the long-term success of your small-group ministry. Starting out correctly by having others on board and a team mentality is essential. The ministry is organic, as I have said throughout this book, meaning it grows on its own, in sometimes unpredictable ways. It is best not to lock yourself into a certain process, but be flexible, in order to allow God to tweak the ministry for his work.

Throughout this book you have had thoughts generated about your current ministry and your mind raced with all the things you want or need to do—but the time you have to offer each of these is limited. Life happens. Ministry must go on. And then there is number 19 on every job description: *other duties as assigned*. Let me encourage you!

Of all the things we've discussed, *connecting in communities* must be more about real life than theory. No matter the size of your ministry, issues will always arise. The organic nature of small-group ministry will almost always guarantee you a job, because someone has to continually develop plans to respond to or solve the issues. But beyond your job security, there must be a discipleship response to the issues. At the same time you must continue to be a learner, whether as a small-group pastor or small-group leader.

Consider how God has developed his plan in your life and ministry up to this point. Consider where you are spiritually and what preparation you need to take the next step on the journey.

There are several timeless principles that should govern your evaluation of what to do next. Read through each one and prioritize them according to your current situation. In a few months, come back and reevaluate. You will never solve all the issues, but you can continue to grow as they arise.

Prayer

As the disaster-relief leader approached the house, he could see a man standing in the front door. It was an older gentleman whose house had just became accessible after the flood. The disaster-relief leader introduced himself and said he was from LifePoint Church and had a team coming out tomorrow to help him clean up his house. The gentleman said, "I knew someone from that church would be here." He had been praying for help from the community to help him get his house back in order.

Prayer should be the first on the list of timeless principles for each of us. As we journey into something new or deeper into what we do, prayer will give us answers to direct our path. Prayer is not something that we should do just when the floodwaters are approaching; we should *pray continually* (see 1 Thessalonians 5:17). Praying daily by name for each small-group leader, coach, or member will impact the ministry far more than our reading, talking, or planning.

Praying in the small group is important also. It is very common for people to be uncomfortable with prayer, especially praying out loud in front of a group. Helping people get comfortable with talking and listening to God is a major step in helping them move on the journey to being Christ centered. Spending time one-on-one with people in your group and allowing them to pray will build their confidence in praying alone or in the group. Help them gradually increase their responsibility in regard to leading in prayer.

Objectives

He and his wife came early to church one Sunday so we could meet and talk about their group and how our team or I could help them. He talked about their recent studies and a little bit about each family in the group. She told the God story of the group, how it began, what God had been doing in the lives of the people, and how they had met a couple on Wednesday night at the church and had invited them to the group.

Then he looked at me and said, "But Eddie, we do not have a service project for our group. We have done a few one-time things, but nothing as an ongoing basis. We need something that will help us look beyond ourselves."

He knew the objectives of a small group, not because I gave him a checklist as he walked in; not because I asked him about discipleship, community, and service. He knew because we continually hold these up for our leaders to shoot at. He knew, as the leader, what success was and what his group's weakest area was.

I have talked a lot about having a target and a plan. I use the word *objective*, but it matters not what word you use—it is the fact that you have a clear target in mind. Objectives can keep groups from becoming closed or confused about how to define success. Narrow down your goal and help groups know the goal for small groups.

Share the Load

She was new to small group. She had been raised in Sunday school and as an adult had attended a women's Sunday school class for several years. But now as a wife and mother, she'd branched out and brought her husband to a small group. She and her husband quickly became committed to the group and I felt they were ready for a little more leadership opportunity. Since we continually laughed at some of their stories about travel and events, I asked her to plan the next party for our group. After a few initial questions, out came her calendar book and she was taking the lead. Now she and her husband not only feel a part of the group, they belong—they *own* the parties for the group.

No matter where you are in the small-group process, you must focus on sharing the ministry of small group at all levels. Many years ago I learned this principle the hard way. I was youth minister at a church that loved to have big events for teens. However, the local community also offered a lot of events for teenagers to choose from, so attendance could be sporadic. We started giving every teen and leader a job for the events—bringing drinks or chips, taking tickets, setting up equipment, decorating, and so forth. This immediately conveyed ownership of the events and increased attendance. Sharing the load has been a part of my ministry practice ever since; it's a way to mentor, involve others, and share the responsibilities for discipleship and growth in leadership.

Consider how you can share some of your tasks—weekly or monthly—in a way that will apprentice someone for his or her next step in ministry. It will bless you both.

Relationships

The text read, "Is our small group meeting tonight?" I quickly replied, "Yes, at 6:00 p.m. at my house." This text was from the babysitter for our small group and she had used the word *our*. I was so excited that I called our entire group and told them she finally felt that this was more than a job — she was part of our group!

She was sixteen years old and had a desire for God's leadership and direction in her life. She was involved in our church as much as she could afford. As a teenager who'd just received her driver's license, she had to get a job to pay for a car and gas to put in it. Her first job was babysitting for a few families at church.

Our small group was made up of young families who had a lot of kids. We struggled with how to take care of the kids during our small-group meeting. The wives would take turns going to another room or backyard and entertaining the kids while the other lucky adults got to have Bible study.

Then it dawned on one of the parents that a girl at church was a good babysitter and might be willing to babysit during the Bible study time. Our first question was how much to pay her. We discussed it for a while and came up with a plan.

Although our small-group time can go two or three hours total, she would babysit our kids for only the one hour of Bible study. That kept the costs down and enabled all the wives to participate in the study. We still struggled with how much we should really pay her. Finally we discussed paying her five dollars per family, no matter the number of kids. She was able to walk away with twenty-five or thirty dollars per week for one hour of serving. She was happy and always did a great job.

I still felt we should do more. I did not feel good about just giving her cash and letting her play with the kids for an hour. There had to be something more we could do for her. There had to be a way for this to be more than a job. She was always faithful to the group, showed up on time, and would hang around after her allotted time, just to talk with adults and be part of the family.

Finally we came up with a plan that had much more impact in her life for a longer period than the cash would last her. We had an idea that would influence her life for a long time by helping disciple her. We decided to pay her way to our church's summer student camp. When I told her what we were planning to do, she and her mother almost cried. Her small group had just become a little more like family and made a memory for the next generation.

Small-group ministry is about relationships—how you add new people, how successful the coach is, and how well your group grows. As the relationships deepen, the feeling of family grows. You can get to the point that you know where other members of the group are at almost any moment of the day. I often talk about my group and how we have become family, texting or calling almost daily. We all know what the others are involved in or praying about. Even the babysitter.

Service

Jason had been part of my last two small groups. He made the jump with me to start a new group of mutual friends who did not attend church very much. About eight months into the group I had the feeling Jason was ready for something more—service, maybe. Other than driving the golf carts in the church parking lot on holidays, he had not individually served before. I asked him if he would consider leading a student small group, guys my son's age. He had already had an impact on my son and his friends. Jason, to my surprise, said, "I think I might like doing something like that. Let's talk more about the details."

In the results of the Reveal research project by Willow Creek, "the top-ranked factors in all three movements include the word 'serve.' Serving is the most catalytic experience offered by the church. It's the serving experiences that demonstrate increasing levels of spiritual influence; and it's worth noting that serving those in need (versus serving in a church ministry) tops the list of catalysts"[1] on the spiritual journey.

Your first six months in a new small group are very similar to your first six weeks of dating. A lot of smiles, weird feelings, politeness, and avoidance if anything's uncomfortable—all are present. The "it"—the community feel that is like family—of small group may not exist. Yet.

You probably formed your small group based around content, a churchwide campaign, or a common interest. To get your group started, you may have asked people you did not know very well to be in your small group.

Your new group obediently met for the allotted amount of time for the campaign. "It" may have been hard to develop. Some of the couples haphazardly attended. Other couples became good friends over the few weeks.

How can you get "it" in your group? Serving together could be the very thing that will unite your group.

Some of the best lessons a person learns are in the hard times of life or in those projects that require you to work alongside someone else. One of these lessons I have watched lived out in small-group life is the "common enemy."

We have seen groups struggle to stay together, with several excuses. However, when offered a service project or faced with an enemy (cancer, divorce, troubled children, house fires, loss of job), the group gets a new burst of life and desire to attack this project or enemy together. Your group may be struggling for direction and unity. Watch for opportunities for your group to serve as you drive to work today, or as you drop off your children at school, or as you sit in worship this week. Your views of life and situations change when you help others. Your view of yourself changes when you help others.

Refrigerator Rights[2]

When I visit someone in his home, whether it is for a party or a meal, I quickly learn about the family. I immediately notice if they have a pool (and how I can get invited back if they do). The decorations, the lawn, the landscaping, and the pictures on the walls all speak volumes about the family values and lifestyle.

Hosting your small group in a home is much more casual and provides an open-ended atmosphere. Opening your home for small group allows others to see into your life a little deeper and increases the opportunity for transparency, accountability, and community. This may be the reason some families will not host a small group. On the other hand, this is the very reason we encourage small groups to meet in homes.

After several years of working in small-group life, we have seen several reasons for people not opening up their home. Most of these reasons can be categorized in one of the following issues: size, design, value, transparency, or decor. You may hear: "My house is just not big enough," or "Our house is not child-proof." Others say, "My house is not as fancy or as expensive as most of the people in our small group."

The benefit of rotating locations of the meetings is to get to know others in your group at a deeper level as you see how they live and what they like. However, for some this level of transparency cannot be expressed, because the feeling of being family isn't deep enough to reach that depth of trust.

Another benefit of rotating locations is to take the workload off the same family week after week. My kids don't like to vacuum, but when we host small group in our home, they vacuum and clean. I love hosting small group at our house, but for my family, it's a lot of work. Build the refrigerator rights by hosting once in a while; it helps every family.

Here are a few pointers that may help in rotating locations:

- **Scheduling further into the future.** If your group does not communicate well or often via text or e-mail, you need to plan ahead even further. Life happens and schedules are made well in advance, but small group seems to be like Sunday dinner: we know fifty-two weeks in advance that Sunday is coming and we will want lunch. But most of us stand around after worship in the hallways discussing where to go for lunch. Plan ahead. First discuss individually with some potential families that may host, then open up discussion in a meeting.

- **The size of the group may be hindering hosting.** When a group gets too large (varies by group and perception), people are fearful of opening their home. A group of six or eight couples with kids makes potential hosts think they need a large space—but everyone does not have to have that comfy seat. We are family. It is like Thanksgiving at Mamaw's house: Get your food when you can. Take a seat where you can. But most of all, enjoy the family!

- **Ask in private, in advance.** Look at the potential host and listen for concerns. People do not like to say no to their friends, but deep concerns will allow them to. Be compassionate and empathic as you encourage them and do not push this issue.

Discussion

I spoke at another campus on Sunday night, which was also our small-group meeting night. We were in the middle of a six-week study on understanding the Bible. That night we were to finish the section on the Old Testament—not an easy night to hand off to someone to lead. I reviewed the material and wrote four discussion questions. I gave the questions to one of the group members (no official apprentice had been named yet). I e-mailed the entire group and told them I would be absent but they could discuss these four questions for the study that night. As I walked through the door about halfway through the small-group time, I saw eight adults digging through their Bibles and study guides looking for answers and talking about the northern and southern kingdoms.

If I had not practiced the open discussion in the small-group Bible study time over the preceding months, I don't think this meeting would have happened.

Of course, building on the discussion model is not just so the group can handle your absence. It is about increasing the feeling of family, the transparency, the potential apprentice, *and* when you're absent, the group keeps going.

Discussion, not lecture: When leading a group, our tendency may be to talk and avoid silence. It is easier to control the room and not worry about tough questions when we lecture. But small group must be about discussion, sharing, learning about each other. It is not about the information but the relationship. An important part of discipleship is the discussion, the fellowship around the snack table or a cup of coffee after the study.

Apprentice

Stanley was new to Christ. He was a researcher who analyzed everything. No decision was arrived at quickly. He and his wife joined a small group soon after attending the church. Stanley became friends with the small-group leader, who asked him to be his apprentice. Stanley said yes, and the journey began.

He branched out and started his own group about twelve months after becoming an apprentice. Due to his leadership skills he was asked to be a small-group coach. He said yes, and the journey deepened. Two years after his coaching began, Stanley called me and announced that he felt the call to ministry. He was not sure what exactly that meant, but God was leading him to finish his college degree and move into ministry full time.

I wish this were the story for how smooth every apprentice situation will be—but we know that is not the story in most cases. However, had the small-group leader not asked Stanley to be his apprentice, what road might God have used to get Stanley's attention? How can you help people hear the call to ministry? What can you do today to help small-group leaders in the future? Apprenticing is not about the here and now, but could help others hear the call for future generations. The ultimate example of sharing the load is apprenticing.

Start Asking Questions

Coming from a field in which I had many years of experience and was very knowledgeable — as a counselor working with Major League Baseball players for the Rangers and Cardinals — I felt that when I began serving as a part of the Small Groups Network I needed to keep up my professional persona and pretend that I knew the answers about small groups. I didn't. And when I decided to take off my "expert mask" and start asking questions, I really learned and made some close relationships in the network as well.

— Mark D. Mehlig, Calvary Church, St. Louis, Missouri

Organic

Small-group ministry is organic in many ways. The group experience itself is organic as people grow to be more like Christ and more like family. But it is not only about the small groups; it's about your ministry and your growth as well. Several new developments and opportunities will arise as the small-group ministry continues to grow across the country and around the world.

Some of the opportunities that I used to view as unimportant are now vital to our ministry. For example:

- **Conferences** are still one of the best ways to help your small-group ministry team and potential leaders catch the vision of small groups. Each year we budget to take a few potential leaders to a large conference away from our city. The experience of attending such a conference in many cases cannot be replaced by an in-house or even local training event. The seminars, speakers, and workshops all share a different view of ministry and help expand the vision for your team.

  Another benefit to conferences away from your church is the travel to and from the event. I have spent hours learning, discussing, and customizing the information from the conference with our team on the way home.

Conferences have developed over the years and are more targeted and longer lasting. Most conferences will leave you with more questions and information to digest than you have time to deal with while present at the conference. A couple of ways we have been able to continue the learning are conference calls and small-group networks.

- **Conference Call**. In addition to conferences, I read a lot of books and continually review websites. We also participate in conference calls, a very inexpensive and convenient way to learn from others. In a recent conference call that lasted all of forty-five minutes, I learned from small-group leaders in Pennsylvania, Canada, Colorado, California, Minnesota, Tennessee, Wisconsin, Connecticut, and Texas. This conference call connected leaders from across the nation in follow-up to a recent small-groups conference. Most of us had never met each other. Our situations were vastly different in size of ministry and years of experience, yet we were dealing with the same issues, and in some ways we felt like old friends.

- **Small-Group Networks**. I spent several years in the same church as minister of education. I did not know any colleagues in my area because I had too much tunnel vision and too many workaholic tendencies. I missed a lot of knowledge, help, prayer, and encouragement because of my lack of networking.

Most conferences now help you connect after the conference by linking you to local networks. Participants can opt in to an e-mail list and are then contacted by the local network representative. I have joined, and encouraged my team to join, one of these networks in my local area.

The Small Group Network[3] in Nashville is comprised of directors and pastors; they meet quarterly to discuss small-group ministry and encourage each other. The Network is important to keep us informed but also to combat Satan's two lead-off hitters, *isolation* and *fear*, the two most powerful weapons in keeping us from connecting to God and experiencing the fullness of life God offers.

We know this network continues to encourage, educate, and build community for each of the participants. We are also seeing the benefits of the network lived out in each of our churches as we learn new ways to connect people to small groups and help them grow to be more like Christ.

YOUR SPIRITUAL NEXT STEP

Church-growth consultant Carl George asks, "How are you getting in the way of what you want to happen?" It's an excellent question. I have learned from my ministry experience—and mainly from my personal experience—that most of us know exactly what our next spiritual step is, whether that be to move, stop, start, or avoid something in our lives. The problem rests not in the lack of knowledge, but in self. Self, ego, fear of loss, giving up control—all are concepts that keep us from stepping out on faith in our spiritual journey to be more like Christ.

Where are you on the path? How do you go about discovering your next step for your life? For your ministry? The question "What is my spiritual next step on the journey to be more like Christ?" is not always an easy one to answer. Small group, worship, prayer, and obedience all play a part in hearing God as he gives us direction. The small-group discussion has opportunity to assist hundreds of individuals in this search.

As we began our search for what studies to offer—which was simply a reflection of our attempt to help people move on the journey—LifePoint hosted a three-day fast and sacred gathering. We met nightly, Sunday through Tuesday. I know this may sound crazy to you—and until Sunday night about halfway through the first night of the gathering, it did to me too. Not eating, but praying; the calmness of office life due to no e-mails and preferably no phone calls; the lack of television; no baseball practice or studying for the next game—for three days, these things helped me focus on my life, my direction, my cause for doing all I do at such a hurried pace! It gave me a chance to . . . *quit*! *Everything*! . . . and just have conversation with God. In this time I was challenged inside myself to seek my spiritual next step.

Our small-group leadership team felt much of the same peace. We knew this was bigger than just a fast or a time to decide on curriculum. This was a time to seek not only our individual next step but also the focus and clarity of our division. In the end we agreed that the expectations and objectives of our ministry would drive all our work. They would become the benchmarks for groups, activities, training, and curriculum.

You may have never participated in a spiritual fast. You may have not taken or been given the time to be calm, to focus, to search for your next step in life. The thought of not eating for a few days may be foreign to you. I want to challenge you to take the time to experience what God has in store for you. *Stop! Quit!* Whatever speeds up your life, stop it for a few days.

Ask yourself *What is my spiritual next step*? God has been trying to share with you the plans and dreams He has for you (see Jeremiah 29:11). He loves you! He has bigger plans than even you can dream.

Small-group ministry is not about finding the easy way out, it is about discipling people and enabling a system that puts people in biblical community so that they can better hear, respond to, and live out God's plan for their lives. It is about living in biblical community so that the stories you have read in this book can become real in your life and ministry.

Now that you see what small groups can do, your future in small-group ministry may have just gotten a little larger. Your vision must include seeing those around you, those God has entrusted to you, your group, and those under your influence brought closer to Christ—and also seeing that they grow and develop in their specific calling to lead the next level of ministry around the world. No longer will you just lead a small-group study; you are developing missionaries for the kingdom, who will take Christ where you may never go. You are no longer talking about this week or last week, but next year, the next generation, the next community, the next country, the next continent that God is calling you to impact. Tonight or this week in your small-group ministry, don't look at it as you have in the past. Look into the eyes of those in your church or in your group and catch a glimpse of the picture God is beginning to paint in their lives. Let your mind move to following Christ as a lifestyle, not a program on your calendar. I can now say that for this glocal (global and local) impact, "Truly I was born for this!"

FIVE PRACTICAL STEPS FOR . . .

Your Ministry:

1. After reading this book, what is your spiritual next step?
2. What do you need to pray about, spend time researching, or whom do you need to schedule a meeting with for the next step in your ministry?
3. Do you have an answer for one of the biggest questions concerning small-group ministry (What do I do with the kids?)?
4. Which timeless principle is your ministry practicing best?
5. In which timeless principle is your ministry the weakest? What will you do to improve this area in the next thirty days?

Your Small Group:

1. Determine your spiritual next step and ask a friend to help you stay focused.
2. On which timeless principle does your group need to improve?
3. What ideas did you gain from this chapter or book that will help you or your group disciple the next generation?
4. What are some of the deeper issues in your small group that you need to discuss with your small-group pastor or coach?
5. Decide on a service project that your entire group could get excited about and schedule a date to serve.

ACKNOWLEDGMENTS

Thank you: Gerald Sharon, David Johnston, Tony Wotkiewicz, Jenny Sanders, Barry Sneed, Travis Buchner, and the Small Group Network, for the mentoring, support, and coaching in small-group ministry so I could even have such a story to tell.

For all of my friends and small-group leaders of LifePoint Church who shared their God story so I could have a story—Kevin Fleet, Charlie Mitchell, Jason Arnold, Wes Burney, Dennis Carwile, Randy Roth, Pat Hood, Jamie and Larry Winnett, Joel Sturdivant, Bob Goins, Benjamin Bright, Charity Smith, Jon Frazier, Brad Bynum, Bret Auner, Marcus Mister, Chris Vondohlen, my small group, and the wonderful people of LifePoint Church—thank you.

APPENDIX

Following are items specifically mentioned in the text, organized by chapter in which the reference occurs.

CHAPTER 2

If you are planning to add a small-group ministry alongside your current Bible study structure, here is a sample calendar that we have practiced for several years. This plan not only walks you through adding groups, it allows you to involve some of your current leadership.

Sample Calendar for Adding Small Groups to Current Structure: Year One

Pray for 10 to 20 percent of your current leaders, whether that be Sunday school leaders or group leaders to be willing to try a new teaching style.

May–July

Start a small group on your own, meeting two times a month. Tell the stories often. This could be a turbo group or small group.

July–August

Have meals with the open/interested 10 to 20 percent to enlist them to pilot the new style this fall.

September–December

Watch for God to work in the pilots. If you did a turbo group, have participants start their own groups now.

October

Take potential leaders of small groups to a small-groups conference. Tell your stories of small group. Meet weekly with turbo graduates about their groups.

January–February

Challenge conference attendees to meet neighbors or friends who might get involved in small group with them. Start their groups.

February or April

Take leaders to a small-groups conference with focus on enlarging the infrastructure of your organization.

March–May

Tell stories and offer opportunities to connect with a small group.

June–July

Continue to enlarge the infrastructure for small-group organization, adding leaders and coaches.

August–September

Conduct a churchwide campaign to add people to small groups. Challenge people to invite unchurched friends. Challenge Sunday school to participate in the campaign.

More and more churches are adding a "discovery" or "information" session for visitors or for those desiring to join the church. Sometimes it is a required session for new members. For LifePoint, Discover LifePoint is that class. Here are some main points for this class that may help you design one for your church.

Discover LifePoint

Discover LifePoint is the best first step for becoming involved and connected, as it reveals the mission and motivation behind LifePoint Church. The one-time class is offered every month at LifePoint campuses. Attendees spend an hour with LifePoint staff and discover helpful information and get questions answered. Attendance at Discover LifePoint is a required step for membership to LifePoint.

LifePoint Core Values

We will honor the WORD.
We will value PEOPLE.
We will live in UNITY.
We will pursue RELEVANCE.
We will strive for EXCELLENCE.
We will remain FLEXIBLE.

Characteristics of a Disciple

At LifePoint Church, we are on a journey and want others to join us as we pursue God and seek to introduce others to him. We never ask our members to do more than the Bible clearly teaches. We only expect our members to do what the Bible expects every Christian to do.

A. WORSHIP Exodus 20:3; John 4:24
   Corporate/Together in a service. Offered on Sunday mornings.
   Private/Personal: daily devotions or appointments with God.
B. BIBLICAL COMMUNITY Acts 2:42
   LifePoint accomplishes this expectation mainly through small groups, on- or off-campus.
C. SERVICE 1 Peter 4:10; Ephesians 4:11-12; 1 Corinthians 12:12

Using the passion, gifts, and talents God has designed you
with to serve ministry on-campus or missions: local, state,
national, or international.

D. INFLUENCE Acts 1:8

LifePoint Church expects every member and attendee to
invest in the unchurched.

E. GENEROSITY Malachi 3:10

Not to the church, but to the Lord.

CHAPTER 3

Every small group needs to have guidelines under which everyone in
the group agree to operate. Here is a sample small-group covenant that
you can adapt for your ministry.

Sample Small-Group Covenant

It is important that your group agree on a covenant. Setting these
guidelines is the first step toward real Christian community. The
following example can help you get started.

We will meet on _____ at _____ o'clock.

Child care will be provided by_____.

Food will be _____.

We agree to . . .

Discipleship

- Make our meetings a priority
- Have Bible study at least two times per month
- Pray for the lost
- Worship personally in quiet time and corporately
- Develop future leaders

- Allow everyone to participate in discussion
- Challenge each other on our path to growing to be like Christ

Community

- Host monthly socials and quarterly influencing events
- Allow group members to hold us accountable to the commitments we make
- Share the work load of small group
- Call on each other at any time
- Respect each other's opinions
- Keep discussions confidential unless permission is granted

Service

- Encourage members to serve each other as needed
- Serve God through on-campus opportunities of LifePoint Church
- Serve the world by praying for, encouraging people to go, and/ or supporting participants of mission experiences
- Serve the community by identifying a project that our group will adopt

CHAPTER 4

The following card is a sample of the info card used at LifePoint. This card is completed by anyone interested in connecting with a small group.

Small-Group Info Card

Name_____

Today's Date _____

Age Range (circle one) 18–24 25–30 31–40 41–49 50–59 60+

Street Address_____

City_____ Zip _____

E-mail _____

Phone (H)_____ (M)_____

Marital Status: Married | Single

Children: Yes | No   Ages _____

Helpful Info:

Fielder's Choice

Neighborhood ministry is not limited to subdivisions. We include sports and hobbies in our neighborhood ministry. Here is the definition of our baseball sports ministry, Fielder's Choice, to give you an idea as to how you might capitalize on resources within your congregation.

Fielder's Choice is a group of baseball enthusiasts who lead player and coaches' clinics. Founded and led by former MLB pitcher Charlie Mitchell, Fielder's Choice uses the combined abilities and knowledge of baseball veterans to help players become the best they can be. Starting with foundational drills and squads, Fielder's Choice helps participants gather the correct form and techniques to better enable them to enjoy the game. It's comprised of leaders who represent various levels of baseball, including Little League, high school, college, minor leagues, and Major League Baseball. Each of our leaders are actively pursuing a growing relationship with Jesus Christ as they allow him to work through them and use their abilities to share his love.

CHAPTER 5

A small-group host at LifePoint is someone who facilitates a group of people through a churchwide alignment series for six weeks.

Expectations of a Small-Group Host:

- Attend host orientation before launch day.
- Prepare for each week's study by attending worship and praying through the study.
- Personally invite four couples or eight singles to your group.
- Membership at LifePoint is not required to be a host. (Membership is required to be a small-group leader.)
- It is very important that you show up prepared for each meeting.
- Pray for each member by name during the week as you prepare for the session.
- Ask members to help you prepare by praying and attending worship.
- Honor everyone's time by starting and ending on time.
- Let God teach you and direct you as you study his Word.
- Find ways to challenge the group to apply the lesson during the coming week.

Host Interview (Things to Consider About a Potential Host):

- Is he growing in Christ? In the Word, worship, praying daily?
- What is his calling? Does he know what God's vision is for him?
- Does he have character?
- Will he be compatible with others? Are people drawn to him? Does he have friends?

- Will he stay committed to a group? Has he let other ministry areas down?
- Is he teachable and obedient to authority?

Once the six weeks are completed, most hosts decide to continue leading the group. At that point they must be members of LifePoint and are required to complete the next development course, Leadership Development 1.

How Can I Become a Small-Group Leader?

- Be a Christ follower
- Be baptized
- Regard the Bible as God's authoritative guide for your life
- Be a member of LifePoint
- Hold to the essence of LifePoint
- Agree to come under the GroupLife structure
- Complete one of the following:

  - Attend a host orientation session
  - Be in a small group for three to six months or participate in a turbo group
  - Apprentice alongside an existing small-group leader

We have designed three structures for small-group ministry. The development, ministry, and sharing structures are described below.

Development Structure

- Attend annual training opportunities
- Attend a minimum of two small-group luncheons per year
- Meet face-to-face with your coach at least three times a year
- Have an apprentice in training when possible

Ministry Structure

- Grow your group as God directs
- Model discipleship, community, and service to your group
- Stay in contact with members weekly
- Share the load by encouraging members to use their gifts and passions in the group
- Develop an apprentice to start a new group in six, twelve, or eighteen months
- Guide the group to minister to each other as needed

Sharing Structure

- Share stories with your coach and friends monthly
- Share enrollment and attendance with office weekly
- Share struggles with your coach as often as needed

CHAPTER 7

How to Host a Neighborhood Easter Egg Hunt

The steps to hosting an Easter egg hunt for your neighborhood are simple. This is an easy opportunity to get to know your neighbors and have a fun, safe event for the kids, and it only takes a small amount time to carry out. Our hunts usually cost less than fifty dollars to complete.

1. Consider the streets around you. Identify the area you want to invite.
2. Invite some neighbors to be part of the core group that will help you host the hunt.
3. Design a flyer (or e-mail, if you have a directory of your

neighborhood), copy it, and have your core team distribute it to your neighbors. Ask each neighbor to bring a dozen or two plastic eggs filled with individually wrapped candy. Let them know that your team will hide eggs on Saturday morning. Always start ten to fifteen minutes after the advertised time. In my ten years of hosting neighborhood Easter egg hunts, I have learned that there are *always* two or three families who are late.

4. The core team will meet on Friday night to stuff eggs. Many families will donate candy but may not have time to stuff the eggs. Saturday morning, hide eggs, set up the prize table, and keep kids out of hiding areas until ten minutes after the advertised start time. Some of the core team will manage the hunt while others work the crowd. Many parents will stand around, drink coffee, and introduce themselves to their neighbors while the kids hunt eggs. This is the time for some of your core team to be meeting others, listening for stories, and discerning next steps in the relationships with neighbors.

5. Encourage everyone to attend the next event, gather names of people who would like to help with next event, and then clean up.

The entire event lasts about an hour and a half. Our work begins at 10:00 a.m. to hide eggs and set up tables. The Easter egg hunt will be at 11:00 a.m. Then we clean up and take down tables and go home by 11:30 a.m.

SUGGESTED READING LIST

Donahue, Bill and Greg Bowman. *Coaching Life-Changing Small Group Leaders: A Practical Guide for Those Who Lead and Shepherd Small Group Leaders.* Grand Rapids, MI: Zondervan, 2006.

Donahue, Bill. *Leading Life-Changing Small Groups.* Grand Rapids, MI: Zondervan, 1996, 2002.

Donahue, Bill and Russ Robinson. *Walking the Small Group Tightrope: Meeting the Challenges Every Group Faces.* Grand Rapids, MI: Zondervan, 2003.

Fay, William. *Share Jesus Without Fear.* Nashville, LifeWay, 1997.

Frazee, Randy. *The Connecting Church.* Grand Rapids, MI: Zondervan, 2001.

George, Carl F. *Prepare Your Church for the Future.* Grand Rapids, MI: Revell, 1991.

Gladen, Steve, *Small Groups with Purpose: How to Create Healthy Communities.* Grand Rapids, MI: Baker, 2011.

Hawkins, Greg and Cally Parkinson. *Follow Me: What's Next For You?* Barrington, IL: Willow Creek Association, 2008.

Howerton, Rick. *Destination Community.* Nashville, Serendipity House Publishers, 2007.

Hybels, Bill. *Just Walk Across the Room.* Grand Rapids, MI: Zondervan, 2006.

Maxwell, John. *Developing the Leaders Around You.* Nashville, Thomas Nelson, 2003.

Miller, Dr. Will and Glenn Sparks, PhD. *Refrigerator Rights: Creating Connections and Restoring Relationships*. Barrington, Barkley, Willow Creek Association, 2002.

Myers, Joseph R. *The Search to Belong*. El Cajon, CA: Youth Specialties, 2003.

Rusaw, Rick and Eric Swanson. *The Externally Focused Church*. Loveland, CO: Group, 2004.

Search, Bill. *Simple Small Groups: A User-Friendly Guide for Small Group Leaders*. Grand Rapids, MI: Baker, 2008.

Stanley, Andy and Bill Willits. *Creating Community: Five Keys to Building a Small Group Culture*. Sisters, OR: Multnomah, 2004.

Warren, Rick. *The Purpose-Driven Church: Growth Without Compromising Your Message and Mission*. Grand Rapids, MI: Zondervan, 1995.

Winseman, Albert L. *Growing an Engaged Church: How to Stop "Doing Church" and Start Being the Church Again*. New York, Gallup Press, 2009.

NOTES

Chapter 1

1. Randy Frazee, *The Connecting Church* (Grand Rapids, MI: Zondervan, 2001), 141–147.
2. Andy Stanley and Bill Willits, *Creating Community* (Sisters, OR: Multnomah, 2004).
3. Rick Rusaw and Eric Swanson, *The Externally Focused Church* (Loveland, CO: Group, 2004), back cover.
4. You can read more about the Heifer Project at www.heifer.org.
5. *Christmas with the Kranks*, from a novel by John Grisham, screenplay by Chris Columbus (Sony Pictures Home Entertainment, 2004), dialogue transcribed by the author.
6. Andy Stanley and Bill Willits, *Creating Community* (Sisters, OR: Multnomah, 2004), 20.

Chapter 2

1. E-mail to author from P. K. Spratt, minister of education, Jersey Baptist Church, Columbus, OH; used by permission.
2. Steve Gladen, Todd Olthoff, and Brett Eastman, *Spiritual Health Assessment and Spiritual Health Planner* (Lake Forest, CA: Saddleback Church, 2005).
3. Lyman Coleman, speaking at Small Group Summit, LifeWay Church Resources, Nashville, February 2010. Notes taken by author.
4. These are derived from Bill Hybels, *Courageous Leadership* (Grand Rapids, MI: Zondervan, 2000, 2002), 80–81.

5. Bill Donahue, *Leading Life-Changing Small Groups* (Grand Rapids, MI: Zondervan, 1996, 2002), 184.

6. Dr. Will Miller and Glenn Sparks, PhD, *Refrigerator Rights* (Barrington, IL: Barkley Publishing Group, Willow Creek Association, 2002), xii.

Chapter 3

1. E-mail to author from Rich Smith, minister of discipleship, First Baptist Church, Ellisville, MO; used by permission.

2. Rick Warren, *The Purpose Driven Church* (Grand Rapids, MI: Zondervan, 1995), 95.

3. Bill Search, *Simple Small Groups* (Grand Rapids, MI: Baker, 2008), 16.

4. E-mail to author from Dr. Virgil Grant, pastor, Eastside Church, Richmond, KY; used by permission.

5. Albert L. Winseman, *Growing an Engaged Church* (New York: Gallup Press, 2009), 25.

6. Bill Donahue, *Leading Life-Changing Small Groups* (Grand Rapids, MI: Zondervan, 2002), 184.

7. Greg Bowman, speaking at Small Group Summit, LifeWay Church Resources, Nashville, February 2010; notes taken by author.

8. Adapted from Donahue, 107–108.

9. See www.churchteams.com/ct/ © 2000–2009.

10. Rick Howerton, *Destination Community* (Nashville: Serendipity, 2007), 43.

Chapter 4

1. For information about Saddleback's HOST strategy, see Steve Gladen, *Small Groups with Purpose: How to Create Healthy Communities* (Grand Rapids, MI: Baker, 2011), chapters 12–13.

2. Adapted from Rick Warren, "Eight Reasons to Join a Small

Group," www.turningpointolympia.com/Download_Files/small
_groups_eight_reasons.pdf, accessed August 15, 2010.

3. "GroupLink," LifePoint Church, www.lifepointchurch.ord/
grouplink, accessed August 15, 2010.

4. E-mail to author from Mike Medlin. Used by permission.

Chapter 5

1. John Maxwell, *Developing the Leaders Around You* (Nashville:
Thomas Nelson, 2003), 47.

2. Bill Donahue, *Leading Life-Changing Small Groups* (Grand
Rapids, MI: Zondervan, 1996, 2002), 184.

3. Carl George, interview with the author, March 2010.

4. Jon Weiner, at a presentation during the Regional Point Leaders
Retreat, November 2009, transcribed by the author.

5. "The Best Case Scenario Guide for Community Group Leaders,"
adapted from unpublished conference handout materials by Bill
Search (Southeast Christian Church, Louisville, KY) from Steve
Gladen (Saddleback Church, Lake Forest, CA). Used at a
Purpose-Driven Small Groups Connection Event attended by the
author.

6. Steve Gladen, Todd Olthoff, and Brett Eastman, *Spiritual Health
Assessment and Spiritual Health Planner* (Lake Forest, CA:
Saddleback Church, 2005), 3.

7. Maxwell, 1–2.

8. Charity Smith, ministry assistant to GroupLife, LifePoint
Church, Smyrna, TN. Used by permission.

Chapter 6

1. Greg Hawkins and Cally Parkinson, *Reveal: Where Are You?*
(Barrington, IL: Willow Creek Association, 2008), 37.

2. Hawkins and Parkinson.

3. Hawkins and Parkinson, 36–37.

4. Steve Gladen, Todd Olthoff, and Brett Eastman, *Spiritual Health Assessment and Spiritual Health Planner* (Lake Forest, CA: Saddleback Church, 2005), 3.

5. E-mail to author from Rick Howerton. Used by permission.

6. E-mail to author from Carl George. Used by permission.

Chapter 7

1. Greg Hawkins and Cally Parkinson, *Reveal: Where Are You?* (Barrington, IL: Willow Creek Association, 2008), 37.

2. Dr. Will Miller and Glenn Sparks, PhD, *Refrigerator Rights* (Barrington, IL: Barkley Publishing Group, Willow Creek Association, 2002).

3. You can access this resource online at http://pdsgn.wordpress.com.

ABOUT THE AUTHOR

EDDIE MOSLEY is executive director of GroupLife at LifePoint Church, a multisite campus in Smyrna, Tennessee. Active in the small-groups movement, Mosley has led conferences across the United States and is a sought-after speaker known for his passion to help pastors and staff develop strategies to implement small groups in their churches. He has written numerous articles for SmallGroups.com and LifeWay Church Resources and serves as Regional Point Leader for the The Small Group Network. Mosley is a graduate of Middle Tennessee State University, where he received his bachelor of business administration. He also holds a master of divinity degree from Southern Seminary in Louisville, Kentucky. Mosley and his wife, Lisa, have two sons and reside in Middle Tennessee.

The Message Means Understanding

Bringing the Bible to all ages

The Message is written in contemporary language that is much like talking with a good friend. When paired with your favorite Bible study, *The Message* will deliver a reading experience that is reliable, energetic, and amazingly fresh.

DATE DUE
